James Moses Nichols

Perry's Saints

Or, the fighting parson's regiment in the war of the rebellion

James Moses Nichols

Perry's Saints
Or, the fighting parson's regiment in the war of the rebellion

ISBN/EAN: 9783337148423

Printed in Europe, USA, Canada, Australia, Japan

Cover: Foto ©ninafisch / pixelio.de

More available books at **www.hansebooks.com**

PERRY'S SAINTS

OR

THE FIGHTING PARSON'S REGIMENT IN THE WAR OF THE REBELLION

BY

JAMES M. NICHOLS

BOSTON
D. LOTHROP AND COMPANY
32 Franklin Street

Copyright, 1885, by
D. LOTHROP AND COMPANY.

ELECTROTYPED BY
C. J. PETERS & SON, BOSTON.

MEMORIAL SKETCH OF THE AUTHOR.

To the rising generation the war of the rebellion already seems more like a romance than a reality. One by one the active participants in that momentous period of the nation's history are passing away. In a few years there will not be a veteran left to tell the story of his own experience on field and in camp. Hardly had the writer of the following pages completed and revised his work, and placed the copy in the hands of the publishers, when he, too, was summoned to join the great army beyond. That he had a touch of the rare quality which we call heroism, as well as fervent patriotism, is sufficient reason why the reader should know something more about him than is disclosed in the faithful and comprehensive record of his army life contained in this volume.

James M. Nichols was born in Haverhill, Mass., in 1835. His early education was received in the public schools of his native town, and he prepared for college at Phillips Academy, Andover, Mass. He graduated at Williams College in 1857, having been a fellow-student with President James A. Garfield. The storming of Fort Sumter fired his heart with patriotism, and he was soon among his own townsmen actively engaged in enlisting a company which was at once consolidated in another organization. He then went to New York, and was commissioned as a lieutenant in the 48th regiment, but afterwards rose to the rank of captain. During his three years of service Colonel Nichols was second to none in that famous regiment in thorough devotion to duty and in the display of soldierly qualities. On several occasions he was in command of the regiment, and led it through many a fiery ordeal with courage and ability. In recognition of these services he was brevetted successively major, lieutenant-colonel, and colonel. In private life Mr. Nichols was frank, manly, impulsive, sympathetic, and an earnest Christian. To these qualities were added musical gifts and a rare power in conversation, which made him a delightful companion; while to those who knew him best, his thorough genuineness, and the nobility of a nature which scorned everything narrow and mean, made him the trusted and beloved friend. He died suddenly, July 1, 1886, from the effects of disease contracted in the service. He was tenderly borne to his last resting-place by comrades from the Grand Army of the Republic, and he has left behind as the inalienable possession of his sons the legacy of a pure, upright, and useful life.

PREFACE.

The following narrative is, for the most part, a transcript from journals kept by the writer during his three years and more of service in the army of the Union. Facts, experiences, and observations, were noted down from day to day, whether we were in camp, in garrison, or in the field, and are given to the public in the hope not only of affording pleasure to those who have never shared in such experiences, but of correcting erroneous impressions in regard to the real life of the soldier. Those who served in the army, I feel assured, will recognize the truthfulness of the picture of army life.

JAMES M. NICHOLS,
Brev.-Col. U. S. Vols.

HAVERHILL, MASS.

CONTENTS.

CHAPTER I.
Causes of the War. 13

CHAPTER II.
Colonel Perry. Formation and character of the regiment. Luther B. Wyman, Esq. 19

CHAPTER III.
Camp Wyman. Incidents of camp life. Lieutenant Elfwing. Fête Champêtre. Departure for seat of war. List of officers. In camp near Washington. Off for Annapolis. General Butler in Maryland. Attitude of Governor Hicks. Waiting at Annapolis. Colonel Perry's last sermon. Journey to New York. Return of contrabands. Departure for Fortress Monroe. . . 32

CHAPTER IV.
At Fortress Monroe. General Viele's talk. Weary waiting. Off at last. Order of sailing. Storm. Horrors of the voyage. Vessels lost. Off Port Royal. Tatnall's Mosquito fleet. Bombardment of Hilton Head and Bay Point by navy. Surrender. Captain Drayton. Landing of troops. First camp on Confederate soil. Foraging. Negroes' account of bombardment. Inspection and review. The sutler. Thanksgiving. . . . 48

CHAPTER V.
Expedition to Port Royal Ferry. Progress up Broad River. Colonel Perry acting brigadier-general. The rebel yell heard for the first time. The regiment's first baptism of fire. The old horse. Night on the field. Return to Hilton Head. Object of the expedition. Presentation of flag to the regiment. Off for Dawfuskie. Southern homes. Preparatory work by Major Beard and others. Building batteries on Jones and Bird Islands. Mud and malaria. Reconnoissances and midnight wanderings. . . . 73

CHAPTER VI.
Planting batteries on Tybee Island. General Gilmore. Listening for the opening gun. Bombardment of Fort Pulaski. Watch-

ing the contest from Dawfuskie. Surrender of the fort. Its
appearance after the bombardment. 94

CHAPTER VII.

Camp life at Dawfuskie. Scheelings and his "leetle tog." High
living. Effects of malaria. Discussing the situation. Emancipation order of General Hunter. Lincoln the emancipator. John
C. Calhoun and nullification. Ordered to Pulaski. James
Island expedition. A sad failure. Shouting service of the
negroes. 100

CHAPTER VIII.

The wreck of the sutler's schooner. Its consequences. The
death of Colonel Perry. His character. Action of officers.
Sent to New York. Lieutenant-Colonel Barton promoted.
Detailed on recruiting service. General Mitchell commander
of the department. Expedition to Bluffton. Blockade-runner
Emma. Confederate ironclad. Back with the regiment. Its
condition. Bluffton again visited. Ravages of war. . . 112

CHAPTER IX.

Expedition to Coosawhatchie. Landing at Dawson's planta-
tion. March to Coosawhatchie. Ambuscade. Firing on
Confederate train. Confederate prisoners. Destruction of
track. Retreat. Peril of Lieutenant Corwin. Lieutenant
Blanding wounded. Pocataligo expedition a failure. Perilous
voyage back to Pulaski. Confederate weapons. Yellow fever.
Death of General Mitchell. His character. Review of
Coosawhatchie. 124

CHAPTER X.

At Fort Pulaski. Changes at Dawfuskie. Amusements. The
pride and taste of the soldiers in fitting up their quarters.
Mosquitoes and other pests. Thanksgiving celebration. Incidents of garrison life. Flag of truce. Confederate ironclad.
New Year's Day. Mr. Logan's account of the condition of
things in Savannah. Prices of provisions, etc. Resignation
and departure of Chaplain Strickland. Inspector-General Townsend's and Colonel Green's opinion of the regiment. Flag of
truce. Interesting interview with Adjutant-General Gordon
and Lieutenant Styles, of the Confederate army. Formation
of negro regiments. Our theatre. Building a steam launch.
Deserters. Capture of blockade-runner. Effect of garrison
life on the regiment. Capture of Confederate ironclad Atlanta. 132

CHAPTER XI.

Good-by to Fort Pulaski. At St. Helena Island, under General
Strong. Billinghurst and Regua battery. Folly Island.
Masked batteries. Attack on Morris Island. Killed and
wounded of the regiment. Captain Lent. Capture of Con-

federate batteries. Building batteries. Hot work and little rest. Completion of batteries. Assault on Wagner. Badly managed. Terrible losses. General Strong. Negro soldiers. Their effect upon the Confederates. After the assault. The shelling by the Confederates. Incident 157

CHAPTER XII.

Back to the regiment. Off for St. Augustine. The duties of provost-marshal. The quaint old city. Its pleasant people. Two months of rest. Lieutenant Ingraham. Back to Hilton Head. The regiment reunited. Visit to Morris Island. Captain Eaton. Fort Wagner and its reminders. Lieutenant-Colonel Green. 178

CHAPTER XIII.

Relations between the 47th and 48th regiments. Re-enlistment of veterans. Court-martial. Departure of veterans on furlough. Expedition to Florida. Battle of Olustee. A great blunder. Heavy losses. Admirable conduct of the troops. Dr. Defendorf. The retreat. Return of veterans. Sergeant Thompson. At Palatka. Expedition into the country. Dunn's Creek. Its marvellous beauty. Ludicrous scenes. Good-by to Palatka. At Gloucester Point, Va. A happy change. Shelter tents. General Grant. Army of the James under Butler General Terry. 188

CHAPTER XIV.

Bermuda Hundred. Company E as skirmishers. Battle of Chester Heights. Couldn't resist the temptation. Company E fighting on its own account. Bad predicament. Company E did nobly. More fighting. In sight of Richmond. Confederate sharpshooters cleaned out. Battle of Drury's Bluff. Company E again in a bad spot. Wonderful examples of discipline and soldierly conduct. General Terry to the rescue. Retreat. Back to old quarters. Captain Lockwood. . . 205

CHAPTER XV.

Assigned to 6th corps. On the way to the Army of the Potomac. A dreadful march. At Cold Harbor. Trying situation. Assume command. A gallant charge. Grand success. Severe losses. Driven back. Lack of support. Incidents of the battle. The demoralized general. Further account of Cold Harbor. Occupying the Confederate line. A sad picture of war. An uncomfortable situation. Relieved. Close work. Change of base. Grand but perilous movement of the army. The old church at Jamestown. 222

CHAPTER XVI.

Back to Bermuda Hundred. A running fight. Destruction of railroad. Kindness of Major Young and General Terry.

Ordered to charge. A happy escape. President Lincoln and General Butler. Ordered to attack Confederate line. Recalled. Captain Fee and others killed. Picket-lines at Petersburg. Sanitary and Christian Commissions. Mine explosion. Our losses. Major Swartwout. Effects of malaria. 241

CHAPTER XVII.

On duty at the front. Strange sickness. General Grant under fire. Captain D'Arcy. Battle of Strawberry Plains. Splendid behavior of the regiment. Lieutenants Tantum and Sears picked off by Confederate sharpshooters. Other losses. The excited officer. Hurried retreat. Captain Taylor. The greeting of General Terry. A night's rest. On picket duty. Sad condition of the regiment. Expiration of term of enlistment. Disaffection. Severe duty. Artillery attack on Petersburg. Out of the service. 254

CHAPTER XVIII.

Discharge of old members of the regiment. Attack at Chapin's farm. Partial success. Condition of the South. New recruits. In winter-quarters. Thanksgiving Day. Resignation of Colonel Barton. His long and faithful service. Tenth and Eighteenth corps united. Expedition against Fort Fisher. Second expedition against Fort Fisher. Gallant charge and capture of the fort. An important event. Other successes. March to Wilmington. Pursuit of the Confederates. Their surrender of Union prisoners. Their condition. On the march to join Sherman's army. Sherman's grand march to the sea-coast, and its results. Grant's operations ending in surrender of Lee and his army. With Sherman's army on the march for Johnston. Announcement of surrender of General Lee. Continued pursuit of Johnston. Lincoln's assassination. Its effect on the army. Surrender of Johnston. 264

CHAPTER XIX.

A general review. Change in condition of the regiment. Barrett as provost-marshal. Delicate question. Colonel Coan. Gradual disbandment of the army. Discharge of the 48th. Some personal explanations. 289

CHAPTER XX.

Special references to some of the officers of the regiment. Remarks upon prominent questions before the country. Finis. 295

LIST OF ILLUSTRATIONS.

	PAGE
FORT SUMTER,	15
THE UNION VOLUNTEER REFRESHMENT SALOON,	38
FORTRESS MONROE,	49
MAP OF A PORTION OF "SEA ISLANDS," SHOWING "PORT ROYAL,"	53
PLAN OF THE BATTLE AT PORT ROYAL HARBOR,	56
FORT WALKER,	58
FORT BEAUREGARD,	59
DRAYTON'S MANSION,	60
POPE'S HOUSE AT HILTON HEAD,	62
LIVE OAK GROVE AT PORT ROYAL,	63
NEGRO QUARTERS,	67
OBSTRUCTIONS IN SAVANNAH RIVER,	80
FORT PULASKI,	96
BREACH IN FORT PULASKI,	97
THE PLANTER,	109
HEADQUARTERS OF HUNTER AND MITCHELL,	129
MARTELLO TOWER, TYBEE ISLAND,	139
NEW IRONSIDES AND MONITORS,	149
THE INTERIOR OF FORT SUMTER,	153
SIEGE OF CHARLESTON,	159
NOISELESS HAULING OF THE GUNS,	165
BOMB AND SPLINTER PROOF,	167
FORT WAGNER AT POINT OF ASSAULT,	168

LIST OF ILLUSTRATIONS.

FORT WAGNER, SEA FRONT,	171
THE SWAMP ANGEL BATTERY,	173
A FLORIDA SWAMP AND JUNGLE,	198
GENERAL GRANT'S HEADQUARTERS AT CITY POINT,	201
LINE OF DEFENCE AT BERMUDA HUNDRED,	211
PICKETS ON DUTY,	214
FORT DARLING,	217
GENERAL SMITH'S HEADQUARTERS, COLD HARBOR,	223
POSITION OF GENERAL SMITH'S COMMAND AT COLD HARBOR, VA.,	227
BATTERY AND CHURCH TOWER. SITE OF JAMESTOWN,	239
BATTERY NEAR DUTCH GAP,	244
DEFENCES OF RICHMOND AND PETERSBURG,	opposite 246
OUTLINE OF THE CRATER AND MAGAZINES,	249
ARMY'S HUTS AT CHAPIN'S FARM,	265
OFFICERS' QUARTERS, CHAPIN'S FARM,	267
PONTOON BRIDGE AT JONES' LANDING, NEAR DEEP BOTTOM,	269
INTERIOR OF FORT FISHER,	275
PLAN OF LAND AND NAVAL OPERATIONS AT FORT FISHER,	opposite 276
MOUND BATTERY NEAR FORT FISHER,	279
M'LEAN'S HOUSE, THE PLACE OF LEE'S SURRENDER,	285
PLACE OF JOHNSTON'S SURRENDER TO SHERMAN,	287

PERRY'S SAINTS.

CHAPTER I.

Causes of the War.

For years the irrepressible conflict had been going on. From the halls of Congress to the remotest hamlet of the North, the subject of slavery — its national wrong and its individual cruelties — was the constant occasion for irritating debate and violent denunciation. The wall of separation between the North and the South was slowly but steadily building. In the North there had grown up a settled determination that the territorial limits of slavery should be extended no farther, and that the relation of master and slave should not exist in any State north of Mason's and Dixon's line. As this sentiment found frequent expression in active resistance to those laws which sought to protect the master in his rights when travelling or sojourning in the North for purposes of business or relaxation, and in the increasingly aggressive acts of individuals and societies, who sought by all the means in their power to awaken in the slaves a desire for liberty, and to make their way easy for escape from bondage, the conviction became universal at the South that to preserve that institution, regarded as so necessary to their physical and social life, and to establish an effectual barrier to the encroachments of the popular sentiments, not of the North alone, but of the civilized world, there must be separation, and a distinct government of their own.

The conclusion was a logical one, but the territory gained by the blood and treasure of all the people belonged equally to all; and separate existence on the part of the two sections was impossible; and the echoes of the first gun in Charleston harbor, aimed against the Federal flag at Sumter, reverberated among the hills and through the valleys of the North, till every household was awakened, and every arm nerved for the coming conflict. The South had calculated upon divisions and dissensions. It had long

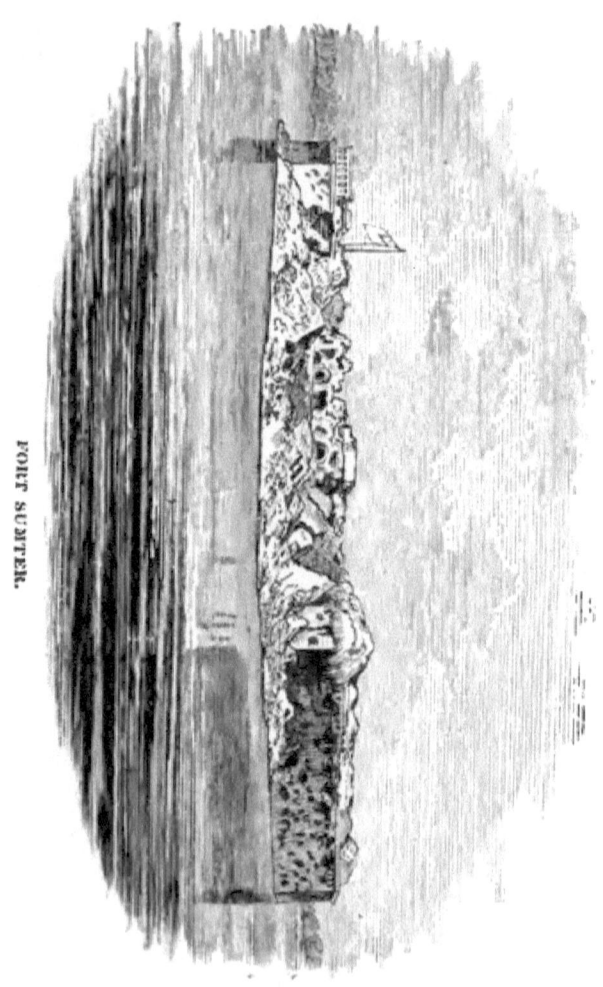

FORT SUMTER.

been maturing its plans and organizing its forces. The head of the Federal government, and many of the councillors and advisers of the administration, were men who either quietly ignored or actively participated in these preparations. The arsenals within its limits, and the fortified points along its coast, with the vast quantities of government property which they contained, were with few exceptions taken possession of without a struggle. Everything at those places in the North where materials of war were manufactured or stored had been ordered to the South. Our navy had been detailed to foreign service, so that at the outbreak of the rebellion there were but two small vessels available for immediate use. Consequently, at the outset, the South possessed many important advantages. But it was mistaken in its conclusions. The unanimity of feeling at the North was hardly less than at the South; and when a new executive sent out his appeals to the loyal States, the answer was immediate. From every city and town, from every village and hamlet, and almost from every household, the word came back: "We are ready for any sacrifice"; "All we have is at the service of the government." The young men put on their armor and gathered themselves together, and the old men lifted their hands towards heaven and blessed them. Wife and mother, though with tears of anguish, said God-speed. The way was dark; but there was no hesitation, no doubt.

CHAPTER II.

Colonel Perry. Formation and character of the regiment. Luther B. Wyman, Esq.

AMONG those to whom the call to arms came with especial force, was the Rev. James H. Perry. He had received a military education from his country, and his country needed his services, and although for many years his mission had been one of peace and good will, his country's needs were an urgent call, and, like the prophets of old, he girt on his armor and prepared for battle.

His was a singular history. Born in Ulster County, N. Y., June, 1811, he early developed great physical and mental strength. That he naturally inclined to a military life, he gave evidence by the fact that, while yet a youth, he was prepared for entrance to West Point, the appointment to which had been promised him by President Jackson for political services rendered by his father. But the wishes of the President were thwarted during his first administration, and it was not until his second election that he secured to young Perry the appointment by sending the warrant to him by special messenger from Washington. In the mean time, the young man had not been idle, but had prepared himself for and entered upon the practice of the law, was married, and seemed settled in his life work. His early tastes, however, and his natural inclinations, decided him upon the acceptance of the appointment.

At West Point his independent and manly character brought him into frequent difficulties. The terms "Mudsills" and "Chivalry," and those of similar import, were, even at that early period, used to distinguish the Northerners from those of Southern birth, and while many of the Northern youth submitted tamely to the assumptions of the Southrons, Perry, who was not of a yielding disposition, and recognized no arbitrary claims to superiority, asserted his right to equality, and maintained it with such courage and ability that he soon became the acknowledged leader of his party, and his strength and skill were often called into requisition to repel attacks, which were the more vicious and dangerous because it was soon apparent that no one of his fellow-students could cope with him on equal terms. In one of these encounters, he barely escaped with his life, having, without suitable weapons, to protect himself against the attack of several, who were well armed and specially prepared for the contest. Court-martialled for participation in this affair, he was sentenced to dismissal. President Jackson not only annulled the sentence, but sent him a letter of commendation.

Soon after leaving West Point, he offered his services to the Texan government, which was then engaged in its struggle for independence. In his endeavor to raise a regiment he was only partially successful, but, with a considerable number of followers, he joined the revolutionary forces, when his natural abilities and military education soon secured to him a prominent place in the little army. We are not able, if space would permit, to give a detailed account of his experiences while in the Texan service. We only know that he held a high and honorable position through the whole struggle, which was finally decided by the battle of San Jacinto.

This proved the turning-point in his career. A short time previous, the forces under Santa Anna had been guilty of an unprovoked and cold-blooded massacre, which so outraged the feelings of the Texan officers that they bound themselves by the most solemn oaths to take the life of Santa Anna, whenever and wherever they should encounter him. The battle of San Jacinto, which secured the independence of Texas, and led to its annexation to the Federal Union, occurred soon after. In this battle, Colonel Perry commanded the Texan left, and, although the Mexican army outnumbered many times the revolutionary forces, in the final charge it was completely routed. In this charge, Colonel Perry found himself opposed by Santa Anna in person, as he thought, and, in compliance with the oath which he had taken, he sought and slew him. Learning soon after that he had been misled by the description given him of the Mexican commander, and that he whom he had slain was a brave and honorable officer, especially esteemed for his high character, he was so grieved and shocked that he left the Texan service abruptly, and all the offices and honors to which he was entitled by reason of his eminent services, and wended his way back to the North, carrying with him a burden of regret and sorrow, from which, in all the varying experiences of his after life, he never fully escaped. A dark cloud overshadowed his life ever after, and at times he seemed to suffer intensely.

Whether it was under the influence of this feeling that he was led to turn so completely from his chosen profession to seek in the ministry a relief from this burden, or subjected to religious influences at a time when he was unsettled in respect to his future, he felt called to this special field of labor, we cannot tell. We do know, however, that in a short time he prepared himself for the work, and for upwards of a quarter of a century devoted himself to it with unwavering zeal. For the most part, his labors were confined to the states of New York and Connecticut, where he occupied some of the most important pulpits of the Methodist-Episcopal Church.

In his new calling he exhibited marked ability, being distinguished no less for his earnest piety, and the zealous discharge of the duties of his office, than for the intellectual vigor which characterized his pulpit utterances. Several times in the course of his ministry, he was selected to represent his brethren in the general conferences of the church, and we cannot doubt the statement which we find in the short sketch of his life, from which we have gathered many facts relating to him, that in the ministry, as in the profession of arms, he found few equals and very few superiors.

At the time of the breaking-out of the war, he was the pastor of the Pacific Street Methodist-Episcopal Church, in the city of Brooklyn, having previously ministered to several others of the most prominent congregations in the same city, in all of which he is remembered with the highest respect and most tender affection. From Dickinson College he received the degree of D. D., and, at the time of our introduction to him, was in the pride of his strength, a man of noble form, of impressive manner, quiet and deliberate in his utterances, and clear and steadfast in his purposes. He had then embarked in the service of his country, and there was no looking back to more congenial employment.

The news of the bombardment of Fort Sumter was received while the conference of which he was a member was in session. Immediately rising in his seat, he said: "I was educated by the government; it now needs my services. I shall resign my ministry, and again take up my sword." His resolution was loudly cheered by the conference. Accepting the command of an organization, which had for some time been recruiting, by authority from the Secretary of War, under the title of Continental Guards, he infused into it new life and character. As companies formed, the regiment took its place as a part of the state quota, and was known as the 48th New York State Volunteers.

Under the State law, all officers, before receiving their commissions, were subject to examination by a military board appointed for the purpose; but, by the courtesy of the Governor, Colonel Perry was allowed to select his own officers, without the intervention of this board; and those whom he selected were sworn into service with the companies as fast as they were formed, without examination. He took personal charge of the enlistments, sending out to those places where he was well known, and as a result, the personnel and morale of the regiment were far above the average of those who entered the service. Indeed, I believe I should not trespass upon the truth, should I venture the statement, as the result of observations extending over more than three years, among troops from all sections of the North and West, that no regiment entered the service of the United States, during the war, which could claim superiority over the 48th, in the character of its officers and enlisted men.

While this result was due, in a large measure, to the influence of Colonel Perry's name and character, more especially in respect to the officers (and we cannot overestimate this influence), to Lieut.-Col. William B. Barton, and Quartermaster Irving M. Avery belongs the credit of originating the organization, and preserving it for a considerable period under circumstances most perplexing and embarrassing. It happened in this wise. Being personal friends, and fired with the enthusiasm which prevailed so generally, they conceived the plan of raising a company, and opened a recruiting station for that purpose. The number of recruits soon passed the limits of their early ambition, and they found themselves with several hundred men on their hands; and the problem as to how to secure them, and at the same time provide them with food and shelter, taxed to the utmost their energies, as well as the pecuniary resources of themselves and friends. Both were young, and with limited means, and their conduct under the circumstances illustrates most happily the generous impulse of enthusiasm which seized upon the people of the North, and for a time shut out all those baser and meaner motives which developed among certain classes during the progress of the war.

By most persistent efforts among the wealthier citizens of Brooklyn, and at the War Department at Washington, and at great pecuniary risk to themselves and their immediate friends, they succeeded so far in the enlistment of men, and the provision for their needs, that they felt warranted in looking forward to a regimental organization. It was then that they cast about for a suitable commander, and were led to approach Colonel Perry, with whose previous history they were somewhat acquainted, with the result as indicated in the foregoing pages.

When we take into consideration the circumstances of these two young men, and the nature and extent of the difficulties they encountered, at one time feeding and housing several hundred men out of their scanty resources, for a considerable period entirely alone and unaided in their work, we feel that they may well take to themselves a full share in the achievements of the regiment, whose birth and early life were so largely the results of their personal exertions and sacrifices.

It is scarcely to be wondered at that the regiment received the appellation of "Perry's Saints," for while many, both officers and men, were very far from being saint-like in tastes or disposition, the term was not altogether without significance. As an illustration, Captain Knowles, of Company D, was both teacher and preacher, when word was received that Dr. Perry was raising a regiment. In a short time he joined him with a company taken from school and parish, of which he became the captain. I remember very well that at the time of the re-enlistment as veterans, when I was temporarily in command of the regiment, a member of that company, a private, came to me to inquire about the terms of re-enlistment, stating that he had a farm worth several thousand dollars, and other property; that he had not been home during his term of service, and he not only wished to see his friends, but to be assured, by personal examination, that his interests were well cared for by those to whom they were entrusted. Satisfied that the terms of re-enlistment would be carried out, and that he would have the furlough promised, he did not hesitate, and as a veteran served faithfully to the end of the war. He illustrates the quality of Company D.

They were called the "Die No Mores," from the fact that while in Fort Pulaski, in their social meetings, the hymn of which this forms a part was their favorite. Poor Paxton! the brave and noble fellow! how fond we were of him, and how much we missed him. Even now I seem to hear him, as he calls to his company, in that terrible attack on Fort Wagner, "Come on, Die No Mores, follow me, Die No Mores." And they followed him, out of the darkness and tumult of that bloody night, into the light and peace of a better life, as we trust; unto Him who hath said to all men, "Follow me, and thou shalt die no more."

But comparisons are odious. Each company in the regiment had its characteristics, and all were excellent; and their officers, almost without exception, were men of education and refinement. In the work of forming the regiment, and preparing it for the field, Colonel Perry was not left alone, but was materially assisted by many influential friends from among his parishioners, who liberally provided whatever was necessary, and did all in their power to lighten his burdens and remove obstacles. The same men were the generous friends of the regiment during its whole term of service. Among them, the most prominent, and the most constant, was Luther B. Wyman, Esq., of Brooklyn, for whom our first camp, at Fort Hamilton, was named, and who will always be held in affectionate remembrance by the members of the 48th. He was a gentleman of high social qualities, of cultivated tastes, of wide influence and considerable means, and his personal friendship for Colonel Perry induced an active interest in the regiment which he was forming. He sought to promote its welfare and secure its rights, as well as to minister to its comforts, to such an extent that he was known as its special friend and patron. While engaged in service at the front, we were assured of a zealous friend at home, whose interest at the State House was powerful to secure us against the intrigues of political managers, who too often found convenient places for friends and followers in the offices which became vacant through the casualties of war.

CHAPTER III.

Camp Wyman. Incidents of camp life. Lieutenant Elfwing. Fête Champêtre. Departure for seat of war. List of officers. In camp near Washington. Off for Annapolis. General Butler in Maryland. Attitude of Governor Hicks. Waiting at Annapolis. Colonel Perry's last sermon. Journey to New York. Return of contrabands. Departure for Fortress Monroe.

JULY 24, 1861, Camp Wyman was formed, at Fort Hamilton, in New York Bay. August 16, the first two companies were mustered into service, and September 15 we received orders to be ready to proceed to Washington. In camp, the time was spent in preparing for the field. The men were regularly drilled, and the officers, by study and practice, endeavored to fit themselves for the duties before them. Not all the time was given to serious work. The men had leisure for recreation, and the officers, as they became acquainted with each other, found suitable amusements while in camp, and were allowed ample opportunity to visit friends, and procure whatever was considered needful or desirable for the campaign before us.

Lieutenant Elfwing, who had enjoyed larger experience than most of us, and withal something of a military education, undertook to initiate us into the mysteries of the sword exercise, which was supposed to be necessary to give us good and regular standing among our fellow-officers; but, fortunately for us, experience proved it to be an accomplishment, rather than a necessity. The only result of Elfwing's proficiency which became generally known, was through the good-natured acquiescence of Colonel Perry, in the proposal for a friendly trial, which occurred while we were in camp on Dawfuskie Island, S. C. We never knew that he renewed the proposal. It was generally understood that, recovering his sword, he wended his way back to his rustic bower, and in the company of congenial friends, found comforting assuagement of his mortification and chagrin, in that indescribable, but most mollifying mixture called puddle.

Elfwing was a noble-hearted, generous man. Educated not only in the schools, but by varied and extensive travel, quick of apprehension, of retentive memory and ready humor, his mind was stored with incidents of personal experience, gathered not only in his native country, Sweden, but in different parts of Europe, as well as through several years of residence in our own country. It was a delight to listen to him, for he had a very happy manner in conversation, and with his friends about him, and fairly engaged in his reminiscent wanderings, took from many an hour its weariness and many a night its sleep. A gallant soldier, he distinguished himself in every engagement in which he participated, and even the loss of a leg did not prevent his continuance in service. When we last heard of him, he was United States Consul at Stockholm, and we trust is still enjoying the honor and comfort of that office, and a more quiet and restful life than when we were together.

As previously stated, September 15, orders were received to be ready to proceed to Washington. The President had urged upon the governors of the loyal states, to hurry forward all regiments as fast as they were prepared for the field, and Governor Morgan, who was always earnest in support of the government, gave personal attention to the matter, visiting the camps, and endeavoring by his presence to arouse enthusiasm, and push forward the troops. He had not succeeded according to his wishes when he visited our camp, and on that account seemed especially pleased, when the colonel assured him that we were ready to start at a moment's notice. Among the members of his staff who accompanied him, was Chester A. Arthur, Ex-President of the United States, remembered by those who saw him at that time as a young man of fine appearance and agreeable manner.

We cannot omit to mention the fête champêtre, on that beautiful evening shortly before our departure, when so many of the friends of the regiment gathered for a few brief hours of enjoyment, before the last good-by was said. All the available resources, within and without the camp, were called into requisition to make the occasion a joyous one: and so it proved. But there is sadness linked with the happy memories of that night. Many a last good-by was said, as the early hours of morning bid the guests depart. Never again did Colonel Perry look on the face of wife or children left behind.

And many a sod, in the valleys and along the hillsides of the South, rests over the silent forms of those who parted from kindred and loved ones then. But no one, at that time, had thought for such things; and when, on the 17th, we broke camp, and took our departure for the seat of war, 964 strong, *we felt only the justice of our cause, and the glory of our purpose.* Fortunate is it that weak human nature does not always stop to measure the probable or possible consequences of its act: a provision of Infinite Wisdom, that we know naught of the future.

The following is a list of the officers when we left Camp Wyman:—

STAFF OFFICERS.

Colonel, James H. Perry.
Lieut.-Col., Wm. B. Barton.
Major, Oliver T. Beard.
Adjt., Anthony W. Goodell.
Surgeon, Joseph L. Mulford.
Asst. Surgeon, Patrick H. Humphries.
Chaplain, William P. Strickland, D. D.
Quartermaster, Irving M. Avery.

LINE OFFICERS.

Co. A.
Captain, Louis H. Lent.
1st Lieut., B. Ryder Corwin.
2d " Asa H. Fergurson.

Co. B.
Captain, Edward R. Travis.
1st Lieut., Nere A. Elfwing.
2d " Theodore C. Vidal.

Co. C.
Captain, James Farrell.
1st Lieut., George McArdle.
2d " Townsend L. Hatfield.

Co. D.
Captain, Daniel C. Knowles.
1st Lieut., James O. Paxson.
2d " John Bodine.

Co. E.
Captain, William B. Coan.
1st Lieut., Frederick Hurst.
2d " Rob. S. Edwards.

Co. F.
Captain, James M. Green.
1st Lieut., Sam. K. Wallace.
2d " H. W. Robinson.

Co. G.
Captain, Anthony Elmendorf.
1st Lieut., Wm. H. Dunbar.
2d " James M. Nichols.

Co. H.
Captain, D. W. Strickland.
1st Lieut. W. L. Lockwood.
2d " C. N. Patterson.

Co. I.
Captain, Joseph G. Ward.
1st Lieut., S. M. Swartwout.
2d " Jas. H. Perry, Jr.

Co. K.
Captain, Samuel J. Foster.
1st Lieut., Sylvanus G. Gale.
2d " Albert F. Miller.

The spirit with which we went forth to service is evidenced by the following, taken from the journal of Melville R. Conklin, a private of Company K. Mentioning the fact that Governor Morgan visited the camp on the 15th, bringing orders to go to Washington, he says: "The order was hailed with joy by every man in camp, as we are all anxious for active duty." The 16th was occupied in packing up, and the Long Roll was beaten for the first time at 2 o'clock on the morning of the 17th, when

the men were formed in line, with knapsacks, haversacks, and canteens, but without arms. These were furnished us when we reached the boat which conveyed us on our way to the South.

It is an interesting fact that Colonel Perry did not give up his work as preacher and pastor until informed of the final order to march, which was communicated to him while he was engaged in the public exercises of the church. Bringing the services to an abrupt conclusion, he started for his command, and never resumed the office of preacher, except on one occasion, which will be referred to hereafter.

Of our journey, we remember only the hospitable welcome at Philadelphia, where we stopped for dinner. Ample provision had been made, and, in common with thousands of others, we have occasion for gratitude to the men and women who, not only at this time, but during the whole war, contributed so generously of their means and personal services, to provide for the wants of the soldiers who passed through their city on their way to the front. At Washington, we were assigned quarters for a single night, in a large brick building on Pennsylvania Avenue, not far from Willard's Hotel. Early the following morning, orders were received to go into camp on the plain back of the Capitol, but, the colonel not being decided as to the exact location, we spent the night without shelter. This was a slight foretaste of the life before us, and in many minds, through that first night of exposure, away from friends, and fairly entered upon new and uncertain experiences, there was a lingering look behind, while through the imagination swept those changing pictures of the future, to which a vague uncertainty or sad foreboding gave a solemn tone.

But the morning light dispelled these dreams, and the novelty of pitching tents and establishing camp for ourselves, kept mind and hand busy. In a few days we changed our location to the immediate vicinity of the other regiments of our brigade, and for the next few weeks our time was fully occupied in perfecting our company and regimental drill. Well we remember the idle speculations of officers and men in regard to our final destination, but while we were soon assured that we were to form a part of the expeditionary corps under Sherman, beyond this, we were completely at fault. And well we might be, since the particular point to be attacked was left to the selection of General Sherman and Admiral Dupont, who were themselves some time in doubt. Colonel Perry soon gave ample evidence of his superior qualifications as an officer, and as a regiment, in a short time, we took the highest rank among the troops with whom we were associated.

October 5 we left Washington for Annapolis, and this movement determined for us, finally, that we were to join the great southern expedition, and that our point of attack was to be in the very centre and hot-bed of—the rebellion—and we were satisfied. There was no thought of the danger from the enemy or the inclemency of the climate, but only of the possibility of being able to strike such effective blows as would give us an honorable place in the final suppression of the rebellion.

At Annapolis Junction, we found part of the troops who had been detailed to protect the railroads, rendered necessary by the attitude of the people of Maryland, who at this time leaned all too generally towards their Southern brethren. Even Governor Hicks, although loyal at heart, under the pressure of the hot-headed secessionists who surrounded him, had protested to the President against the passage of troops through the state, and had it not been for the prompt decision and energetic action of General Butler, the Federal government would have suffered serious embarrassment in this matter. The bayonets of his soldiers opened the way, while their intelligence supplied the means of transportation. Roads were rebuilt, and engines repaired, while troops were stationed along the lines to guard them from interruption. Although Governor Hicks, in the meantime, had recovered his loyalty, so nearly lost, the troops whom we met were still needed to secure its constancy. It was midnight when we reached Annapolis, in the midst of a driving storm, and the deserted college buildings were the only places which promised shelter. To these we were refused admittance by the trustees, but upon the colonel's remarking that he had never seen a lock that a bayonet would not pick, there was no further hesitation. Some other lessons were needed before the people learned the temper of our troops. The answer of the colonel gave a tone to the arguments of the officers when they were refused accommodations by the landlord of the City Hotel, and he acknowledged their cogency. The man who maltreated one of our negro servants assumed a most melancholy attitude of entreaty under the influence of a similar kind of logic, and, if still living, has not forgotten the lessons of that night. Indeed, the whole town was so quickly converted that a delegation was sent to our colonel, as soon as his previous profession became known, to request him to conduct the services in the Methodist church on the first Sabbath after our arrival. Turning to the adjutant, and expressing a disinclination to officiate, he remarked, "You can detail Dr. Strickland, or Major Beard, or Captain Knowles, or Lieutenant Gale, or Sergeant Irvine, or some of the enlisted men." And so he could, for each of those named, and some others in the regiment, were regularly ordained ministers. But the colonel was induced to perform the service, and, attired in full military dress, preached an eloquent sermon.

We soon found many loyal people in the city. The officers were kindly welcomed at the house of Governor Hicks, and Judge Brewer opened his doors with generous hospitality. Orders were strict, and none were permitted to go out of camp without special permission, for no one knew the time for our departure, but such liberty was granted as this uncertainty would allow.

At this time we had a band, but no suitable instruments, and the colonel, knowing that I had reasons for wishing to visit New York once more before our departure on the expedition, kindly detailed me to attend to the business of procuring them. The railroads were then pushed to their utmost in the transportation of troops and supplies, and, finding that the road to Baltimore was so blockaded as to render it very uncertain how long a time the passage to and from that city would occupy, by much persuasion a loyal colored citizen was induced to furnish a horse for the journey.

To any one familiar with the condition of the roads in our Southern states at this period, a journey of thirty miles or more on horseback, through a strange country, would have presented little attraction, and if you add the fact that the sentiments of the people throughout the state were such that Federal troops were picketed along the railroads, and at other points, to guard against the destruction of property, and quell seditious movements, the journey would not have been rendered any more fascinating. Fortunately for my peace of mind, the exact state of things was not fully known by me, and more fortunate still that the horse so quickly developed a better acquaintance with the way than his rider as to be left almost entirely to his own guidance. Occasionally, when a fallen tree had completely obstructed the path, or a dense undergrowth had, from infrequent use, been suffered to obliterate all trace of its presence, or, worse still, when an angle of the road (if it could be dignified by such a term), discovered several paths of equally uncertain character, I admit to a degree of apprehension lest he should take me to some convenient crib, where my welcome would be somewhat warmer than I desired. But if the currents of his life moved rather slowly, they ran in loyal veins, and except for a few uncertain companions who joined me at times, I gave myself up to such enjoyments as the somewhat monotonous way afforded.

Arrived at Baltimore, I left my horse, and proceeded to New York by rail. One day was all the time needed for the transaction of my business, and the following afternoon found me again in Baltimore, anxious to get back to camp, in fear lest the expedition might have sailed, and I be left behind. A short time was taken to collect a few supplies previously overlooked, and as the western sun was just sinking behind the hills, I started on my journey back. I had become better acquainted with the condition of affairs in the state, and scrutinized more closely the countenances and manners of those whom I met, especially of the few who, travelling in the same direction as myself, seemed to insist upon the value of their company to a degree not fully warranted by the suddenness and limited extent of our acquaintance. There was quite sufficient opportunity for reflection during the long hours, that seemed to drag so slowly, as I picked my way in the darkness through those interminable woods, but, like all other things, the journey had its ending. As I approached Annapolis, I was neither shocked nor disconcerted by the challenge of our outpost sentinel, "Who goes there." The orders were strict, and I had no countersign, and it was a relief when the presence of the officer of the guard permitted suitable explanations. These were given while we walked along together towards the camp-fire, and as soon as its light permitted recognition, the exclamations, "Hello, Jim!" and "How are you, Val?" left no room for further hesitation. College and classmates, we had parted several years before, to meet for the first time again under these peculiar circumstances. But the impatience of both horse and rider permitted no lengthened colloquy, and in a few moments I was enjoying the hearty welcome of the colonel and other officers.

October 18 we steamed away from Annapolis in the Empire City, towards Fortress Monroe, the general point of rendezvous for the expedition. Here, by order of the general in command, Colonel Perry was compelled, much against his will, to detail a guard from the regiment to return to slavery a negro found on the transport. Thus the great moral, social, and political movements of the world have always been hampered and clogged by their early scruples. We were never after called upon to perform a similar service.

CHAPTER IV.

At Fortress Monroe. General Viele's talk. Weary waiting. Off at last. Order of sailing. Storm. Horrors of the voyage. Vessels lost. Off Port Royal. Tatnall's Mosquito fleet. Bombardment of Hilton Head and Bay Point by navy. Surrender. Captain Drayton. Landing of troops. First camp on Confederate soil. Foraging. Negroes' account of bombardment. Inspection and review. The sutler. Thanksgiving.

AT Fortress Monroe we remained until the 29th, when, with a fleet of seventy vessels, transports, and men-of-war, we put to sea, and steered for our final destination. I must not forget to mention that, during our stay at this point, there was much talk of a landing; whether for an attack upon some place in the vicinity, or merely for practice in view of what was before us, we never knew, but it gave occasion to General Viele, who commanded our brigade, to call our officers together in the cabin of the steamer, to impress upon them the dangers of the undertaking. It was a bloody lesson, probably thought necessary in the case of simple vol-

FORTRESS MONROE.

unteers, the conclusion of which was that we need entertain no hopes save of a glorious departure to the shades beyond. However, as it is the immediate danger which impresses us most, it was not surprising that we took courage from our hopes, and there was no unusual despondency on our part. Some of the more reckless even ventured to suggest a doubt of the general's information on the subject of our final disposal.

The passage to Port Royal, S. C., which proved our objective point, was a very trying one. The breeze, which at the time of our departure was blowing freshly from the storm quarter, soon stiffened into a gale, such as is seldom encountered even on our dangerous coast, and which threatened the destruction of the fleet. The very admirable order in which we started, with the transports in three columns, covered and protected on either side by the gunboats, was soon broken up, and many of the smaller vessels, which were unfitted for sea service, soon found themselves separated from the fleet, which became completely scattered and in the utmost danger. Some put back to Hampton Roads; one, the Governor, went down, after being relieved for the most part of its crew and the marines who had charge of its freight, and several went ashore and were destroyed by the rebels. During the storm the sealed instructions which had been given to each captain for such an emergency, were opened, and when it abated, the vessels that had weathered the gale quickly gathered at the point designated in the orders.

The discomforts of that voyage, no one can realize who has not been similarly situated. The sea-sickness was trying, but was as nothing compared with the discomfort arising from the close confinement in the fetid atmosphere of the ship, with no means of relaxation and no way of escape. It was a terrible experience. Owing to the great numbers crowded into the vessel, bunks were built all around and in the immediate vicinity of the boiler, and to these the men were very closely confined, until the effluvia from their reeking bodies — for, in the intense heat, all clothing was dispensed with — added to the stench of the filthy vessel, and the irritating annoyance of the vermin with which

MAP
OF A
PORTION OF "SEA ISLANDS,"
SHOWING
"PORT ROYAL."

the steamer was infested, made a fitting counterpart of pandemonium, in point of suffering. Some relief was gained by the transfer, at Hampton Roads, of two companies, with a portion of the freight, to the steamer Matanzas, and a small detail, under Lieutenant Dunbar, to the steamer Belvidere, but it was only slight.

Our grand old colonel, in the height of the storm, securing himself to the mast, spent many hours apparently enjoying the magnificent exhibition of power. Nothing disturbed his equanimity, and his watchful care of those committed to him was never remitted.

November 4 we arrived off Port Royal bar. Under the supervision of an officer of the Coast Survey, soundings were made, and buoys planted along the channel. That night a few vessels crossed the bar, and in the morning the whole squadron moved in, headed by the flagship Wabash. While the soundings were being made, the Confederate Mosquito fleet, under Commodore Tatnall, opened quite a spirited fire, but without effect. And as all the movements of the various vessels were plainly visible from the transports, which were well out of range of the guns, we enjoyed the advantage of witnessing the proceedings, without sharing either the responsibility or danger. On the 6th, the weather was unfavorable, and the attack on

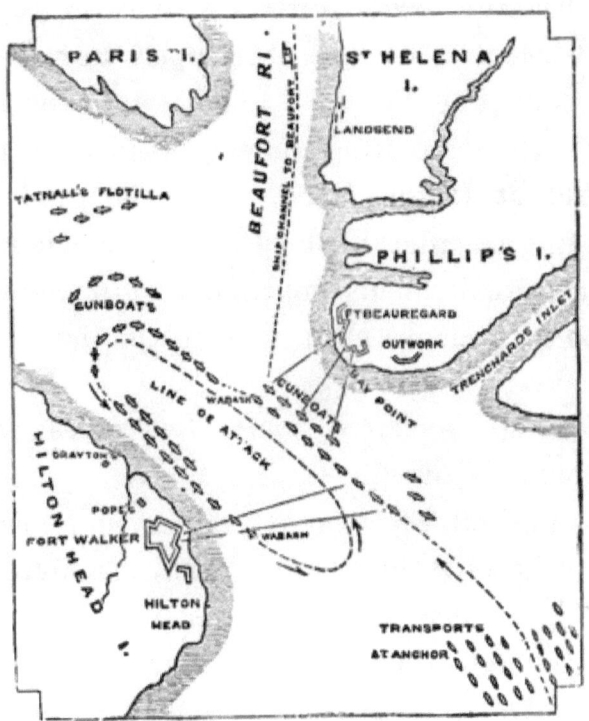

PLAN OF THE BATTLE AT PORT ROYAL HARBOR.

Forts Walker and Beauregard, which defended the harbor on either side, was deferred until the 7th. On that morning the gunboats moved farther in, headed by the Wabash, and the attack on the two forts commenced about 10 A. M. The more effectually to escape the fire of the forts, the gunboats moved continually in a circle, each delivering its broadside as it approached the forts. First, the Wabash poured in its heavy shot and shell upon Fort Beauregard, at Bay Point, as long as its guns bore upon it, and wearing round, opened on Fort Walker, at Hilton Head, while the gunboats, following in order, kept up the cannonade without cessation. This continued until between 2 and 3 o'clock P. M., when the forts surrendered.

Although anchored nearly five miles away, we could follow the direction of many of the shot and shell, especially the latter, and observe their effect. A little after noon, the Mercury, a small gunboat, got on the southerly side of Fort Walker, so near that its guns could not be sufficiently depressed to bear upon her, and from that point was able not only to shell the troops outside of the fort, who were held in reserve, but to throw in so effective an enfilading fire upon the fort itself that its guns could not be served. It was a stroke of impudence which seemed so ludicrous on account of the apparent insignificance of the little craft that the troops on the transports shouted themselves hoarse in admiration of this seeming act of bravado, which, however, proved an important feature of the attack.

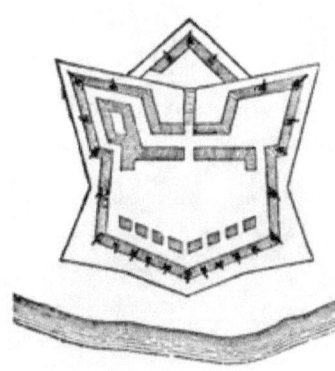

FORT WALKER.

As soon as the fire from Fort Walker ceased, and it was apparent that at least a part of its garrison, with the other forces on the island, was retreating, a flag of truce was sent ashore to arrange the terms of surrender. But it was too late for any conference, as none but the dead and wounded remained, and the Stars and Stripes soon waved the announcement that the first step in the avenging of Fort Sumter had been consummated.

Not a man in the command but felt the significance of that victory. Charleston was nearer now than it had been before, and, in the minds of many, it seemed but a little thing to cover the intervening distance with victorious troops.

The flight of the Confederates was precipitate, and they left behind everything that would cumber a rapid retreat. Fort Beauregard had suffered less from the bombardment than Fort Walker, but the fall of the latter hastened its evacuation, and on the following morning no opposition was offered to its occupation by our forces.

FORT BEAUREGARD.

One fact *in this attack* is worthy of special mention. General Drayton commanded the Confederate forces on Hilton Head, and the home of the family was located on a prominent point near the shore, overlooking the bay, while his brother, Captain Drayton, commanded the gunboat Pocahontas, which participated in the bombardment. Some time afterwards, in company with other officers, I visited the Monitor, which he then commanded, and his grave and saddened demeanor told of the sacrifice he had made in his loyalty to the government.

I know that patriotism is a word with some considered stale and obsolete. Such know little of the temper of the brave men who composed our army and navy during that terrible struggle.

DRAYTON'S MANSION.

For while few were called upon to make such sacrifices as Captain Drayton, the number of those who went to war for hire only was but a small detachment of that great army. And the arguments, even of those unlettered men who formed so large a part of the rank and file, as I have often heard them stated, though clothed in rude and homely language, had in them a degree of intelligence, and were so charged with honesty and sincerity, so backed by courage and fidelity on many a gory field, that it were shame to say the stream of patriotism has run dry. It has not now, and never will, while men have manhood left, honor to defend, homes to protect, good laws and a righteous government to transmit.

November 9 we were all ready to land, having been provided with two days' cooked rations, but for lack of transportation we were detained on board the steamer until Sunday morning, the 10th. The night previous was spent in securing boats and attaching them to our steamer, so that on Sunday morning, as soon as the word was received, we pulled for the shore with a will. At this time, the harbor presented a most animated appearance. The transports were crowded together near the shore, all busy in discharging freight. Boats of all sizes and descriptions were passing to and fro, and horses and other animals were being hoisted from the holds by means of broad bands which encircled them, swung over the sides of the vessels, and gently dumped into the water, to find their way to land as they could, while men stood by ready *to secure them on the shore.* Occasionally the poor distracted brutes, confused by the unwonted sounds, and half drowned by their sudden and unexpected immersion, turned seaward, but were soon brought back.

It was a beautiful Sabbath morning, but with little to remind us of the sacred character of the

POPE'S HOUSE AT HILTON HEAD.

day. After landing, we marched a little way from the beach and remained until about noon, when our camp was located, not far from general headquarters, and we proceeded to prepare the ground for our tents, and establish guards and pickets. Two nights were spent without shelter, on account of the difficulty and delay in landing baggage. After this we settled down to regular work. From ten to twelve each day we had battalion drill, in which the

LIVE OAK GROVE AT PORT ROYAL.

colonel was **very** exacting, requiring the officers to know their duties, and holding them responsible for the condition and drill of their companies. Company drill was from two to four in the afternoon, and dress parade in the evening, often followed by more battalion drill. Details were made for fatigue duty in building entrenchments, an extensive line of earthworks was thrown up as a precautionary measure, and frequently nearly the whole regiment was picking, shovelling, or felling trees to furnish material for the works. There was no idle time, except when a day on picket or other guard duty secured the following as a day of rest.

Having been detailed as officer of the guard the first day in camp, the following day I was permitted by the colonel to accompany a small party bound on a tour of observation. During the day we wandered far away from camp, to the other side of the island, and the afternoon found us on the borders of a large plantation, which proved to be that of a Mr. Seabrook. Approaching the place, we mistook the whitewashed huts of the negroes for tents, and remained a long time in doubt whether to advance or retreat, feeling quite certain that it was a Confederate encampment that we saw. While debating what course to pursue, a stray contraband relieved our apprehensions by informing us that our troops occupied the place. We found on our arrival a detachment of the 45th Pennsylvania, posted there to keep watch for Confederates and prevent foraging. That night we spent in Mr. Seabrook's store, after using the portion of the afternoon that remained to us after our arrival in endeavors to secure some of the cattle, pigs, and poultry, which seemed to be wanting an owner, to which the guard, usually lenient on such points, raised few objections. These came mostly from the quadrupeds and bipeds themselves, and were so strenuous that the result of our efforts was a meagre show of two or three lean pigs, an occasional hen, and an ancient goose, which succumbed to my own personal prowess.

On our way back to camp, the next day, we narrowly escaped arrest, as General Viele had issued an order that all parties coming in from foraging should be deprived of what they had collected and sent to his headquarters un-

NEGRO QUARTERS.

der arrest. My poor goose suffered the fate of the pigs and hens, and no doubt rested heavily on the stomachs of the pickets, if not on their consciences. We were glad to escape with the loss of our plunder.

Supplies were abundant, the negroes bringing to camp whatever the plantations produced, and although General Viele issued an order that everything should be taken to his headquarters, where a general market would be held every morning, no attention was paid to it, and as far as we ever heard, no general market was established.

About a week after the capture of Hilton Head, I was detailed to take command of the Grand Guard, whose headquarters were at Drayton's plantation. The negroes had generally remained here, as well as at the other places within the range of our command, and were encouraged to cultivate the plantations abandoned by their masters. This was important, as the famous Sea Islands formed a part of the territory captured by our forces, and considerable of the cotton remained unpicked, while nothing had been done towards the harvesting of corn, potatoes, and many other products of the soil. Some of the negroes here were owned by Captain Drayton, who had left them in the care of his brother, and no doubt some of the shot from his guns had fallen among his own people. The evidences of the cannonading were manifest all about, and the negroes, when questioned as to its effects upon them, declared that at first they didn't mind the firing, but "when them rotten shot began to spatter about them, they jes' ran for de woods."

The regiment soon became proficient in drill, in spite of the frequent details for fatigue duty, and was regarded as one of the best, if not the very best, in the Department.

November 24 we had a general inspection and review, by Generals Sherman and Viele, in which the brigade marched first in quick, and then in double-quick time, around a circle of some two miles in extent, according to the journal of Conklin, to which reference has before been made. We can all testify that it seemed much longer, with the sand sometimes almost ankle-deep. General Viele perhaps thought us amply paid for the exertion, when he declared that we marched as well as regulars, and were equal to any regiment in the service.

Day followed day with about the same round of duties. We had already become fairly accustomed to tent life, our food supply was ample and good, and the paymaster furnished the means of providing ourselves with comforts and luxuries according to our several positions, or, rather, the amount of pay received. Besides the regimental sutler, who was prepared to furnish anything, from Golden Seal to toothpicks, for a consideration, shops of all kinds sprang up with amazing rapidity, as soon as it became known that this would be a permanent basis of operations, and usually only a short time elapsed after the visit of the paymaster, before his next appearance was looked for with eagerness, even by the sutler, who cultivated a disposition for extravagance, by giving credit to such as seemed likely to regard the obligation. Occasionally, when, too grasping, he became exorbitant in his prices, or in the rate of interest charged for accommodation loans — for too often the offices of banker and sutler were combined — a sudden raid would equalize the account.

At this time, measles and smallpox prevailed to some extent, and from the former several deaths occurred, while the latter was limited to a few cases by the isolation of those attacked.

Thanksgiving and Christmas passed with no observance on the part of the non-commissioned officers and privates, except perhaps a more general application to pick and spade. On Thanksgiving Day, the officers, many of whom had been suitably remembered by friends at home, united their private stores with such good things as could be collected in the vicinity, and indulged themselves in unusual luxuries, forgetting for the time their surroundings, and giving themselves up to the full enjoyment of the day, so far as their duties permitted.

CHAPTER V.

Expedition to Port Royal Ferry. Progress up Broad River. Colonel Perry acting brigadier-general. The rebel yell heard for the first time. The regiment's first baptism of fire. The old horse. Night on the field. Return to Hilton Head. Object of the expedition. Presentation of flag to the regiment. Off for Dawfuskie. Southern homes. Preparatory work by Major Beard and others. Building batteries on Jones and Bird Islands. Mud and malaria. Reconnoissances and midnight wanderings.

THE closing day of the year brought rumors of a contemplated movement. The scene of operations, and their extent, were only subjects for conjecture. Early on the last day of the year, we received notice to be in readiness to march with a number of days' cooked rations, and about noon of that day started for the dock. The expedition was under the command of General Stephens, and two regiments were taken from our brigade,— the 47th and our own,— in addition to those of his regular command. By the middle of the afternoon we were on board of the steam transport Delaware, and on our way up Broad River towards Beaufort, where we anchored for the night. In the early morning, we started for Port Royal Ferry, against which point we learned that the expedition was directed. Several gunboats accompanied us, under the command of Captain Rodgers. Our progress up the river was slow and cautious, until we arrived opposite the plantation of Mr. Adams, where we disembarked.

We were much interested, while on the steamer, in watching that portion of our troops already landed, as they could be distinctly seen, pursuing their winding way through the woods and over the fields, their bayonets glistening in the sunlight. Sometimes they went at slow step, at others in quick or double-quick time. Sometimes they fired, and charged the Confederates whom they encountered, while the gunboats covered them to guard against attack by superior forces, all the time shelling the woods in front of them as they advanced. As soon as landed, we formed in line and moved forward, the two regiments — the 47th New York and our own — under the command of Colonel Perry. Acting as reserves, the duty assigned us was to intercept the Confederate retreat. Very soon, however, orders were received to attack the battery which was found to cover the road over which we were expected to advance, and the 47th was moved through the woods on the right to attack it in flank, while the 48th was to charge in front. Some delay occurred in establishing the position of the 47th, and arranging so that the attack might be simultaneous. Well do I remember the rebel yell, heard for the first time as I was returning from conveying orders from our colonel to the 47th. Accompanied by the discharge of cannon and musketry, it seemed, to my unaccustomed ears, as if the inhabitants of pandemonium had been let loose, and as I rounded the last point of woods which shut out from view the scene of operations, I expected nothing less than a hand-to-hand conflict. Instead, I found the regiment lying quietly down between the furrows of a cornfield, over which the Confederate shot skipped harmlessly. In this way the men were protected while awaiting the final order to charge. This was found unnecessary, for the yell of the Confederates proved only the parting word given while in the act of abandoning the battery, which was speedily occupied by our troops. The guns were removed, and the works destroyed, and we continued our advance towards Port Royal Ferry, where the enemy was known to be strongly entrenched.

At this time two horses had been captured and placed at the disposal of the colonel and his aid, to which position I had been appointed. I have no recollections of the colonel's, but my horse soon gave evidence of manifold infirmities. Three times we rolled over together on that cotton-field, before it was discovered that, with his other weaknesses, he was stone blind, when he was left to tempt some other officer, and I returned to nature's conveyance, sadder and sorer for the experience. That night we lay down on the field, but gained little rest, as the Confederates were known to be in force in the vicinity, and an attack was looked for. The next morning we embarked for Hilton Head, the objects of the expedition having been accomplished, in the destruction of the Confederate works, which were being constructed for the purpose of preventing any forward movement on our part in that direction, and confining us closely within the territory already captured. This was only one of the points which the Confederates proposed to fortify, which were intended not only as a restraint upon any forward movement by us, but also as bases of aggressive operations against us.

January 12 the regiment was presented, through Adjutant Goodell, with a beautiful flag from the ladies of Hanson Place Methodist-Episcopal Church of Brooklyn, of which Colonel Perry had been pastor. That flag has waved over many battle-fields, and is a witness that the 48th never faltered in the discharge of any duty. It is now in the custody of the Long Island Historical Society, having been committed to its charge, with suitable ceremonies, on the evening of April 21, 1881.

January 25, 1862, we broke camp, and marched to Seabrook's Landing, on our way to Dawfuskie, an island bordering on the Savannah River, some four or five miles above Fort Pulaski. That night we spent at Seabrook's, and on the next morning embarked on the steamer Winfield Scott, and proceeded to a place on Dawfuskie called Hay's Point, where five companies disembarked, and at 9 P. M., under the command of Lieutenant-Colonel Barton, started for the other side of the island. Three hours of wearisome marching brought us to Dunn's plantation on the bank of the river. Pickets were established, and sentries posted, and we got what sleep we could. The next day was occupied largely in procuring supplies of food, as everything of that nature had been left on the Winfield Scott. Detachments were sent out in all directions to secure the cattle, pigs and poultry abandoned by their owners on the approach of our troops, and to collect whatever else could be found that was edible. The men were quartered in the houses and sheds, while the officers occupied the family mansion. In the afternoon we learned that the Winfield Scott had been wrecked on Long Pine Island, where the other wing of the regiment remained until taken off by the steamer Mayflower, which conveyed them, with the regimental baggage and supplies, to Cooper's Landing, on Dawfuskie. At this point they remained until February 1, when they joined us, and a permanent camp was established near the borders of the woods, a little way back from the river.

During the interval there was little of severe duty, and all were allowed the largest liberty consistent with proper discipline. Frequent excursions were made to different points on the island, especially to the beautiful residences along the shore. Of these, the most attractive were Munger's and Stoddard's, the former a short distance below us, the latter some miles away, and occupying a commanding position, overlooking the sound. Both gave evidence of large wealth and cultivated tastes, in the character of the houses and beauty of their surroundings, and as we wandered through the shaded avenues, and among the shrubs and flowers, in gardens where roses and japonicas grew in tropical luxuriance, where the air was full of sweet odors, and the eye confused with the multitude and variety of brilliant colors, and remembered that these abodes of happiness and beauty had been abandoned to pillage and destruction, and that wherever our armies penetrated, homes would be broken up, and in the place of comfort would come suffering, and in the place of beauty, desolation, we cursed the madness of those who had brought such miseries on the land.

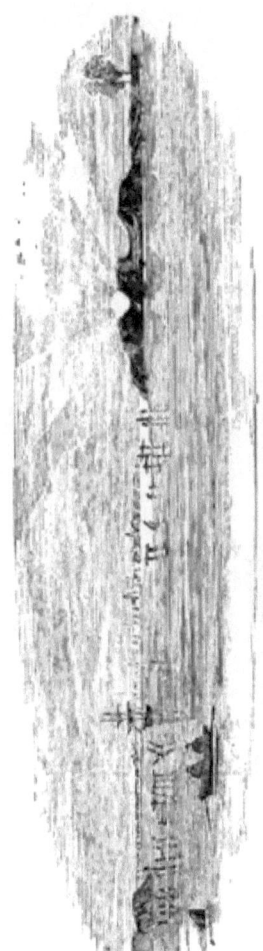

OBSTRUCTIONS IN SAVANNAH RIVER.

While we were enjoying this short season of comparative idleness, active and aggressive operations were going on all about us. Expeditions were planned, obstructions removed from the creeks and rivers where openings were desired, and midnight scouting parties penetrated the surrounding country in all directions, even to the very walls of Pulaski. In all of these, Major Beard, of our regiment, took a leading part, and did most efficient service. As we sat around the fire one evening at Dunn's, he suddenly appeared among us, with General Gilmore, who had already been promoted from the position of Captain of Engineers in the regular army, to that of Brigadier-General of volunteers. They had just returned from the work of clearing the spiles from Wall's Cut, by which a convenient way was opened for our boats to the Savannah. Much of the night was spent in listening to their adventures, but we little knew how intimately connected these were with our own immediate future.

It was not long after our camp was established, before we had our full share of labor and danger. It had been determined to establish batteries on the islands of the Savannah, to cut off communication with Fort Pulaski, and prevent re-enforcements and supplies. The points where these were to be located having been selected, the engineers were ordered to prepare the materials for their construction, and our regiment and a portion of the 7th Connecticut were employed for weeks in conveying this material from the woods to the dock for transportation. Some eight or ten thousand logs, of from ten to fifteen feet in length, and from three to six inches in diameter, were carried a distance of from three-quarters of a mile to a mile and a half, on the shoulders of our men, and, in consequence, many of our best soldiers were ruptured or otherwise injured, and crept out of the service, maimed and ruined for life. Late on the evening of February 9, a detachment under Captain Greene was ordered to report at the dock to complete the loading of the Mayflower. It was raining very hard, but the men worked faithfully until after midnight, when word came from brigade headquarters to take off a part of the load. This was done, and the admirable foresight of the commanding general was fully appreciated, as was manifest from the frequent comments in which the men indulged, which had the merit of earnestness if not of elegance.

At 3 A. M. of the 10th, we started for Jones Island. We were all wet, hungry, and tired. Not expecting to leave Dawfuskie, we had taken no provisions. There was no opportunity for sleep, for, arriving quickly at the point of debarkation, the work of unloading and conveying the materials across the island was pushed forward hurriedly. It was a season of the year when, even in this southern latitude, the sun gave but scanty heat, and the men must needs work lively to keep the blood from chilling. The island was but a deposit of soft mud, into which they sank to their knees at almost every step, while occasionally the logs or planks which they carried were needed to bridge over spots otherwise impassable. During the forenoon, a party was despatched to camp in a small boat, for food, but the supply which they brought was totally inadequate, from the size of the boat and the number to be fed. During the day all the materials for building the battery were conveyed across the island, a distance of about a mile.

While engaged in this work, a Confederate steamer made its appearance, and stopped opposite, and so near to us that every movement of those on deck was discernible. The officers, with their glasses, scoured every point in the vicinity, while we crouched down among the cane-brakes. So long as the steamer remained, we expected a shot from her guns, or a closer inspection by one of her boats, which would have been extremely disagreeable, as the order for detail required us to leave our guns in camp, and there were not six rifles on the island. Fortunately we were not discovered, and the steamer, after a little delay, proceeded down to Fort Pulaski. About this time the guns for the battery arrived, and the general in command of the district, who had arrived with them, declared that they must be mounted before morning. We felt very much like harnessing him to the foremost, and giving him a taste of Jones Island mud, but there were objections to such a procedure, and, instead, we made a platform on which to load them, and prepared to do our utmost. By frequent crossing and recrossing, a way had been sufficiently marked through the canes, but the constant tread of heavy feet had reduced the soft mud to the consistency of oil for a depth of several inches, making a road not perfectly calculated for the transportation of cannon. However, there was no time for hesitation, and placing two planks before the wheels, we united our strength in the task of maintaining them on these planks, while we carefully urged them on, replacing the planks as we proceeded. Woe be it, if, slipping on the greasy mud which covered the planks, as they sometimes did, they buried themselves in the soft embrace of its slimy nastiness. Should it be asked how were they recovered, it would be impossible to tell. We can only say they were, and that with slow and suffering steps we guided, pushed, and pulled them forward, until flesh and blood rebelled at loss of food and sleep, and they were covered up, and we ordered back to camp, to be relieved by others. We had to wait, however, until the relief came from Dawfuskie, and I quote from Sergeant Thompson's journal to show how this second night was spent: "At midnight we covered the guns and endeavored to find some place to lie down in. Found a place, but was soon routed out by the tide. Came to the conclusion to walk the rest of the night to keep warm. Found a twenty-foot plank with four men on it. Jumped on and ran my chance.

Kept moving until morning." This was only the beginning of such labor and exposure, and is it a wonder that so many men, protected from rebel bullets, have come out of such a service as we have here described, to worry through a life of suffering, the effects of which they have transmitted, and will continue to transmit to children and to children's children. The malaria of those mud islands is considered death to any one, even to such as have been acclimated to the South, and their only inhabitant is the ugly alligator.

This battery was hardly established before, pushing across the river, another was planted on Bird Island, farther up, so that, together, they cut off all further communication with Fort Pulaski, by way of the Savannah. An attempt was made to destroy these batteries, but without result, except in the disabling of several of the enemy's steamers, after which we were left in undisputed possession.

The smell of the mud of Bird Island lingers in the nostrils yet, and it is no wonder that in the progress of the work of establishing the battery, at times not a man was fit for duty.

Whiskey and quinine were powerless to stay the effects of such labor and exposure. As a partial protection, our tents were nailed to heavy timbers a foot or more in diameter, snatched from the river as they floated down, while boards were laid across on which we slept, but even then in the high spring tides we were scarcely out of water, and not a spot was dry on the whole island.

During our stay on Bird Island, frequent reconnoissances were made up the river in different directions. One dark night, two boats were sent up the Savannah, on either side of Elba Island, to ascertain if batteries were being planted, which would threaten ours of Bird and Jones Islands. Closely hugging the shore, we worked along cautiously, to avoid being seen by the Confederate pickets. At a distance of some miles from where we started, while the pickets on the shore were plainly visible by the light of their camp fires, one of our men was attacked with a sudden and most sonorous cough. Suspecting that it was intended to stop our further progress, we waited patiently for its cessation, and resumed our progress up the river, until suddenly the sound of voices immediately in front of us gave warning that we had gone too far for safety. Fortunately, the tide had turned, and a single whisper stopped the motion of the oars, otherwise we should not have suffered long from the chillness of the night air. Dropping back with the tide, stopping occasionally to learn more certainly that there were no batteries where they had been suspected, we reached our quarters in season for an early breakfast.

Lying alongside, but extending much farther up the river than Bird, was McQueen's Island, the upper extremity of which was bounded by St. Augustine's Creek, which connected the Savannah with Wilmington River, and afforded a channel of communication with Fort Pulaski by means of small boats. Across St. Augustine's Creek, the telegraph wire connecting the city with the fort had been stretched on tall, heavily constructed spindles. The wire had been destroyed some time before, but the fact that steamboats from Savannah, at some risk from our battery, continued to come down to this point, and seemed busily engaged in some operations near these spindles, determined Major Beard, who commanded on the island, to investigate the matter, and, if possible, to bring away a scow which was known to be lying in that vicinity. The investigation was very proper, but the object of getting the scow we never understood. However, a detail was made, a boat was dragged across McQueen's Island to Wilmington River, and from that point a small party, with a guide supposed to be acquainted with the region, started for these spindles. It was a curious experience, paddling along under the overhanging banks in perfect silence, save when the vivid imagination of some one of the party pictured a Confederate picket from some peculiar conformation of the shore or eccentric growth of bush or shrub, when a word of caution would stay our progress until cooler eyes discovered the deception. One of the party even descried a picket beside its camp fire, whose bright glow shed a clear light upon their waiting figures, but to all the others there was but the blackness of darkness, and we passed on without molestation. The leaky little dug-out, which required constant bailing to keep it afloat, had room for neither rest nor comfort. Hour after hour we paddled along with the incoming tide, vainly hoping to reach the point we sought, every moment taking us farther within the lines of the enemy, and when, at last, completely lost amidst a maze of devious, winding creeks, the tide turned, we turned also, and by marvellous good fortune found our way back before the morning dawn discovered us to the Confederates. Determined to have that scow, and equally determined to have a better knowledge of the country before a second attempt was made, a small party was started one bright afternoon, which, rowing some distance up the river, landed on McQueen's Island, and striking through the canes, made straight for the spindles. We took no notice of the picket on the other side of the island, but kept right on, until, approaching the shore of the creek, the men were held back behind the trees and bushes which grew along the bank, until we could be assured of no special danger. Satisfied on this point, they were allowed to come on, and we gathered along the shore, and endeavored to impress upon each others' minds the direction of the creek, the location of the scow, and the probable means of reaching it from Wilmington River. The order to return had been given, when suddenly the Confederates appeared from behind the timbers of the spindles opposite, and not a hundred yards distant, and from the bushes near, and the order to lie down was given none too quickly to avoid the bullets which came whistling over our heads in close proximity. No one of our party was hurt, and we never received an official report of the number killed and wounded by our return fire. The locality was not sufficiently attractive to induce us to remain until the report was made up. Not only the danger of being cut off by the picket we had passed, but the shells from our own battery soon began to trouble us, for, as it afterwards transpired, one of our number, unaccustomed to the sound of bullets, became so thoroughly frightened at the first discharge that he started for camp by the most direct course, and on his arrival announced that we had been attacked by greatly superior numbers, and that he had been sent back for re-enforcements. Our own battery was soon throwing shot and shell over our heads, much to our discomfort, — for those missiles often make serious mistakes, and fall where they are least intended, — and all that could be spared were preparing to set out to rescue us from the peril to which we were exposed, when our appearance on the river put an end to the alarm. On reaching the island, we found the utmost excitement prevailing, and that every preparation had been made for the reception and care of our wounded. The author of all this confusion was discovered to be suffering the extreme effects of fright, and in a pitiable condition of mental and physical prostration. His youth, for he was a mere boy, shielded him from the consequences of his conduct, which otherwise would have been very serious. He was never permitted, however, to forget the circumstances and effects of his fright. Soon after this I was sent to Wilmington River to intercept the despatch boats, which, we had reason to suppose, found their way to the fort, but although many nights were spent in watching, while the miasma from the swamps was doing its deadly work, penetrating to the very bone and marrow, and preparing many a poor fellow for his final rest, the creeks and rivers which intersected the country in all directions afforded abundant means for avoiding us, and we made no captures.

CHAPTER VI.

Planting batteries on Tybee Island. General Gilmore. Listening for the opening gun. Bombardment of Fort Pulaski. Watching the contest from Dawfuskie. Surrender of the fort. Its appearance after the bombardment.

WHILE we were engaged in the work described in the last chapter, General Gilmore was planting his batteries on Tybee Island, which borders the mouth of the Savannah. These were placed from one to two miles distant from Fort Pulaski, and in the work of establishing them, difficulties were encountered similar to those which so thoroughly tested the skill and endurance of our men on the mud islands above. It required the combined efforts of two hundred and fifty men to drag a single mortar from the beach where they were landed, to position, and as several of the batteries were in plain sight from the fort, the work was largely done at night, until the embankments afforded sufficient protection. The fire from the fort was annoying, but less constant and spirited from the confidence of its commander in its security against the fire of guns so far distant. The value of rifled cannon for siege operations at long range was about to be tested, and while the result in this instance was not entirely to the satisfaction of the commandant of the fort, it fully justified the confidence of General Gilmore, for to him belongs the credit of this achievement, from its inception to its final termination.

By April 6 we became aware that the crisis was approaching, and from that day anxiously listened for the opening gun.

On the 9th, a demand was made for the surrender of the fort, to which the commandant replied, "I was placed here to defend, not to surrender." And he had an opportunity, for on the morning of the 10th the boom of cannon was heard, and from that time until about two o'clock of the afternoon of the following day, the batteries kept up a steady and constant fire. On the first day we could discover little effect, as we watched the progress of the contest from the shore of Dawfuskie, but the next day the frequent clouds of dust arising, especially from the southwest angle of the fort, indicated that progress was being made. During the night the firing had been continued, with intervals of about fifteen minutes, permitting little rest to the garrison, and effectually preventing all attempts to repair or strengthen the fort, and in the morning all the batteries opened and kept up a terrific cannonade, until

FORT PULASKI.

the white flag appeared. Throughout the day the shore was lined with the excited soldiers, especially in the vicinity of Munger's, where a few of us secured places in a large willow tree overhanging the water, and affording an unobstructed view of the conflict. It was not long before a large breach was visible, which gradually widened as the day advanced. The firing from the fort was spirited, but had little effect.

Several times the flagstaff was cut away by our shot, and as often replaced, until about 2 P. M. of the 11th, when the firing ceased. Still, we were ignorant of the exact state of affairs, until an accident revealed the fact that the fort had

BREACH IN FORT PULASKI.

surrendered. A sailing vessel was seen slowly drifting towards it. A steamer followed, apparently for the purpose of rendering assistance, but for some reason she seemed to be unmanageable, and gradually approached and passed the fort without drawing its fire. **By** this we knew that Pulaski was ours, and **another** entrance for blockade runners was closed.

Soon after its surrender, the officers were from time to time allowed to visit it. One bright morning, after the details for the day had been made, in company with several other officers, I was rowed across the river, and spent the day in the quiet inspection of the fort and surroundings. The effects of the bombardment were everywhere visible. Guns were dismounted, bomb-proofs torn and shattered, and the traverses — great mounds of earth for the protection of the gunners, and to guard against the effects of enfilading shots — were levelled almost to the ground. The terre-plein was ploughed and furrowed in every direction, while wide and deep ditches extended across it, to ward off the effects of bursting shells. In many places the blandages, which were heavy timbers inclined against the inner wall, although covered with earth to the depth of three or four feet, were splintered and broken, and large sections of the walls themselves destroyed. The angle against which the heaviest fire had been directed was a gaping mass of ruins, through which at last the shot and shell drove steadily against the magazine, threatening to envelop fort and garrison in one common destruction. It was this danger which compelled the surrender.

CHAPTER VII.

Camp life at Dawfuskie. Scheelings and his "leetle tog." High living. Effects of malaria. Discussing the situation. Emancipation order of General Hunter. Lincoln the emancipator. John C. Calhoun and nullification. Ordered to Pulaski. James Island expedition. A sad failure. Shouting service of the negroes.

FOR the next few weeks our duties were less severe than they had been. The men, by various expedients, had softened down the severer features of camp life. The tents were enclosed in frameworks of poles, which were covered and decorated with evergreens and southern moss, and the officers vied with each other in rendering their quarters attractive. The most pretentious of all were perhaps those of Captain Elfwing, commonly known as Volks Garden, from the fact that, having many friends in the 46th New York, a German regiment, he brought back from his frequent visits to them liberal supplies of their favorite beverage. Several companies of the regiment were stationed at Cooper's Landing and at other exposed points on the island, and on moonlight nights we sometimes made up parties to accompany the officer of the day in his grand rounds. Often these were made occasions for pleasant entertainments at the little outposts. At Cooper's Landing especially we always found hearty welcome, perhaps because we were often the bearers of letters, which, received at headquarters, were sent in this way to those on detached service. Sometimes the colonel visited not only these stations, but other points less carefully guarded, but from which an attack might be possible. At times the officers united in a general mess, but for the most part were divided up into small parties of such as were most congenial, which allowed to a greater extent the indulgence of individual tastes.

The bugler, Anthony Scheelings, must not be overlooked, for at this time especially he was one of the most useful members of our organization. With his little pack of dogs, he was roaming the woods from early morning till evening parade, and seldom returned without an abundance of appetizing game, which he distributed among the messes with impartial liberality. Occasionally a huge rattlesnake contested with him the right of way, but with gun and dogs he was more than a match for beast or reptile. On one occasion however, Scheelings returned from his accustomed ramble with downcast countenance, and upon being questioned as to the cause of his depression, could only answer, "mine leetle tog, mine leetle tog." Some time afterwards, when his grief had lost some of its poignancy, he was able to explain that, while hunting in the marsh, the little cur which was his special favorite, in jumping across a narrow creek, had suddenly disappeared from sight. A huge alligator was discovered soon after, making its way to deeper water, whose movements were hastened by the contents of Scheelings' gun, but the "leetle tog" never returned. The woods abounded with birds and animals, and the numerous creeks and bayous furnished a continuous supply of delicious oysters, and the great sea-turtles, which deposited their eggs along the shores of the river and sound, were often caught too far from their favorite element to effect a retreat. Drill, guard and picket duty were kept up with regularity and constancy, but we look back upon the interval between the fall of Pulaski and our assignment as its garrison as one of comparative rest and comfort. The effects of our exposure on the river batteries now began to be manifest in the pale faces and shrunken forms that crept about the camp, showing that the slow but deadly malarial poison was fastening upon its victims. Loss of appetite, broken sleep, and a general feeling of lassitude, which found but slight alleviation in quinine, were the precursors of more violent attacks, from which many escaped at the time, but whose after life of miserable weakness and suffering has told how deeply were sown the poisonous seeds of lingering disease.

Our mails came with frequency and regularity, and the papers were fairly devoured in the eagerness to learn of operations in the other departments of the army, but the confusion of statements, often half falsehoods and half conjecture, with the reports of deserters, and negroes who found their way through the rebel lines, and the claims of the Southern papers which they brought, altogether, made a jumble and jargon, in which the truth was buried too deeply for any hope of resurrection. The affairs of our own department were equally involved in obscurity and doubt as far as we were concerned, except those matters in which we took part. This uncertainty, however, did not prevent an active interest in and frequent discussion of movements, and that fiction took the place of fact detracted nothing from the hotness of the argument. We fed on what was furnished us, and often built our hopes and theories, fought battles and gained great victories, on the brilliant but groundless conjectures of unreliable correspondents.

From the journal of Sergeant Thompson I learn that on May 12 the emancipation order of General Hunter was read to the troops. While this was somewhat premature, and was annulled by orders from Washington, it foreshadowed the purpose of President Lincoln, who, with a majority of the people of the North, soon came to regard it as a military necessity, and as such the proclamation of January 1, 1863, was issued, by which slavery in this country was forever abolished. Comparatively few slaves were immediately affected, but as our armies penetrated the rebellious states at different points, and the negroes were not only received and protected, but were organized into regiments for service against their late masters, the wisdom of the measure was fully demonstrated. For this act the name of Lincoln, handed down from age to age, will ever be held sacred in the memory of man, as one of the greatest benefactors of the race.

By the middle of May it became manifest that new movements were contemplated in the department. The other regiments on Dawfuskie were gradually withdrawn, and we became interested to learn what disposition was to be made of us. On the 19th the rumor reached us that we were to garrison Fort Pulaski, while most of the troops were to be concentrated in an attack upon Charleston. The 6th Connecticut and the 28th Massachusetts, which had been encamped near us, were ordered away, and we were left almost alone. On the 21st a party visited Hilton Head, where assurances were received that we should form a part of the attacking force, but results showed the falsity of this assurance.

On our return from the Head we stopped at the house on Braddock's Point formerly occupied by John C. Calhoun, and, among the letters scattered about, found many dating back to 1832, which showed the general prevalence of the nullification doctrines at that time, throughout the state. Had the loyalty and energy of President Jackson descended to Buchanan, these years of suffering and loss would all have been avoided. But out of the evil has come such good that few will dare to say that the results are not worth all the sacrifice.

May 23 all doubt in regard to our destination was removed by despatches from Generals Terry and Benham, directing us to proceed at once to Fort Pulaski to do garrison duty. We were very indignant, and felt ourselves grievously wronged, in being placed in what we regarded as ignominious retirement, after having labored so hard, and prepared ourselves so thoroughly for the field; and the officers united in a respectful but spirited protest to be forwarded to the commanding general, but the colonel, knowing better than we, disapproved, and there was no alternative.

On the 25th, the steamer Mattano took seven companies to the fort, leaving E, B, and C on the island, under the command of Captain Coan. At the wharf we were met by General Terry, who directed us to pitch our tents in the most convenient places outside the fort, still occupied by the 7th Connecticut, which was under marching orders. Several days elapsed before the final orders came for the transfer of this regiment to Edisto Island, during which nearly our whole command was constantly engaged in fatigue duty. Company K was detailed to occupy the hulk of an old vessel that had been anchored in the channel, just opposite the fort, and it was not until June 2 that the remaining companies were moved into the fort and entered upon garrison duty. On the same day our troops, under General Benham, landed on James Island, on their way to Charleston. The Stono River had been cleared of obstructions by the navy, and it was supposed that the enemy could not interpose an effectual barrier to our advance. The Confederates were gradually driven back, but finally made a stand at a place called Secessionville, which possessed many natural advantages for defence. On the 15th, preparations having been completed, General Stephens charged the earth-works with his division; but the position was too strong, and he was obliged to retire, with heavy loss. A second attempt was about to be made, with a better disposition of the troops, when General Benham ordered the withdrawal of General Wright's division, and General Stephens was obliged to follow. The losses were very heavy, owing to the nature of the ground. The Confederates were able to concentrate the fire of artillery and infantry upon a narrow neck of land between two marshes, over which our troops must pass to make any substantial progress. They soon received re-enforcements, and this attempt on Charleston was abandoned.

From the first it seemed to be determined at Washington that no important movements were expected in our department. The number of troops was always too small for any large undertaking, and in maintaining a depot of supplies and a place for repairs for the navy, and shutting up the entrances to the coast in our vicinity, and thus limiting the operations of the blockade-runners, we seemed to meet all requirements.

While the attempt at James Island was being

THE PLANTER.

made, I was on the steamer Cosmopolitan, the headquarters of General Benham, and the reports that were continually brought in were heart-rending. Our troops were cruelly slaughtered, and many fell who had been our companions on Dawfuskie and elsewhere. My business, which was with the commanding general, delayed me several days, and while on the boat, one evening, I was much interested by the performances of the negroes on the lower deck. A great many of them had fled from the neighboring plantations and found refuge on the boat, so that the lower hold was crowded with them. At first, my attention was caught by the sound of the soft, plaintive music of a few female voices. The melody was wild and peculiar, differing from anything I had ever heard before, but presently the character of the music changed to the rude and boisterous, in which a multitude of voices were joined. Being interested, I descended to where I could view the proceedings, and was thus able to witness that singular religious exercise called shouting — which bears a striking resemblance to the ordinary worship of the Shakers. At first the dancing was confined to a few, and some leading voice sang the melody, and the others joined in the chorus, but by and by even the old and decrepit men and women seemed seized by the spirit of music and motion, and one by one were drawn into the moving circle, swelling the volume of sound until the vessel fairly shook with the fierceness of the hallelujah. It was a tumultuous, but hearty expression of thanksgiving that the bonds of slavery had been sundered.

CHAPTER VIII.

The wreck of the sutler's schooner. Its consequences. The death of Colonel Perry. His character. Action of officers. Sent to New York. Lieutenant-Colonel Barton promoted. Detailed on recruiting service. General Mitchell commander of the department. Expedition to Bluffton. Blockade-runner Emma. Confederate ironclad. Back with the regiment. Its condition. Bluffton again visited. Ravages of war.

ON the 16th and 17th of June, a fearful storm prevailed along the coast during which a schooner was discovered on her beam ends, on the bar off the west end of Cockspur Island. With much difficulty the crew was rescued, but the vessel became a total wreck, and the cargo, which consisted of sutler supplies, floated ashore on Tybee and Cockspur Islands. Cases of claret and champagne and barrels of beer and wine, were too strong an attraction to be resisted, and the result was that on the 17th the regiment was in a terrible state of demoralization. As soon as the facts were discovered by the colonel, the severest measures were applied. Guards were set along the shores to secure the cargo, and those who were intoxicated were confined in the guard-house and dungeon. The liquor was collected, and locked up in the magazine, and comparative order was restored. It is probable, however, that the excitement and vexation so overcame the colonel as to induce the attack of the following day. It was the first time that the brutalizing effects of the war had manifested themselves in our regiment, and he was grievously wounded. At about three o'clock of the afternoon of June 18, while the colonel was writing at his desk, his pen suddenly dropped from his hand, his head dropped, and scarcely with other sign, *the silver cord was loosed and the golden bowl was broken.* It was a sad day in the regiment. He was so strong — so far above the jealousies of ordinary army life — so just and true — that he was as a rock of defence to such as were in any way dependent upon him. Although holding a subordinate position, we felt that he had no superior in the department, in those qualities which constitute a leader and commander. How well I remember him, as firmly seated on his gray horse, the gift of his ministerial friends and others, he moved about the field at battalion drill, so familiar with the duties of his position as never to suggest a doubt, giving the word of command without effort, but with a power of tone such as I have never heard equalled. Here, as elsewhere, always dignified, always composed. A man to respect, to trust, to obey. It was his misfortune to be confined in a department which furnished so little scope for his abilities, and a still greater misfortune that he incurred the envy and jealousy of those over him. At the time of his death he had applied for leave of absence, and the promise of promotion led him to expect a transfer to some other corps. Had he lived, so large an estimate had we formed of his abilities that we should have expected his rapid advancement to a conspicuous position among the leading generals of the army. As a man he was admired and beloved, for, although reserved and reticent, he did not withhold his confidence, and esteem from such as he deemed worthy of it. Everything relating to those under him received his personal attention, and in cases of discipline, while sometimes severe, he was always just, and when he died the feeling was universal throughout the regiment that the loss we had suffered could never be made up to us. From the time of my first introduction to him, until that morning when I parted from him at Pulaski, never again to see him in life, I recall many instances of his kindness and thoughtful consideration; but they are too personal to be recorded here. Notwithstanding his reserve and his habitual seclusion, except when engaged in active duty, he knew his officers better than they thought, and cared for them better than they knew. As an evidence of this I recall with great distinctness the ride we had together, when we visited various points on Dawfuskie, when he found the rebels were making preparations to annoy or attack us. On our return as we slowly rode towards camp, the conversation turned upon the character and relative merits of the officers of the regiment. He was in a singularly communicative mood, and spoke with unusual freedom. There was no unkindness, no bitterness in what he said, but there was abundant evidence of keenness of observation, and a knowledge of the temper and disposition of those of whom he spoke, and had he lived, no good man would have had occasion to fear him, and no bad man to despise him. His parting words at our last interview in Pulaski, meant more than I knew then, but they were not needed to keep him in my mind, embalmed with loving thoughts and precious memories. We buried him outside the fort, but subsequently his body was removed to Cyprus Hill Cemetery, in Brooklyn; and a granite monument has now been erected above his remains, — by the efforts of James H. Perry Post, G. A. R., and the survivors of the regiment, assisted by the Hanson Place Methodist-Episcopal Church of Brooklyn, of which he had been the pastor. On this is inscribed, in fitting words, the story of his life, his services and sacrifice.

His death left us in a state of some embarrassment. The promotion to the colonelcy naturally belonged to Lieutenant-Colonel Barton, but Major Beard had done much important service in the department, which seemed to deserve recognition, and in addition, his father's relations with prominent men in Brooklyn could command their influence. But he lacked the full confidence of his brother-officers, and his promotion over Lieutenant-Colonel Barton would have been an undesirable precedent to establish, and at a meeting held for the purpose of ascertaining the views of the officers of the line and staff, it was found that we were unanimous in favor of Lieutenant-Colonel Barton, and a paper was drawn up, and signed, requesting from the Governor his appointment. Chosen for the purpose of conveying this, with other letters of recommendation, from Major-General Hunter and Brigadier-General Terry, I hastened to New York by the first steamer, in company with Lieutenant-Colonel Barton, and had the satisfaction of securing all that we desired. From this time until October, being detained in New York, with Captain Farrell, on recruiting service, I must depend upon the journals of Thompson and Conklin, and the sketch recently written and sent me by Major Barrett, for an account of what transpired in the regiment during the interval.

The record is short, and lacking in interesting or important circumstances; occasionally, a flag of truce came down from Savannah, with persons who desired to join their friends in the North. General Mitchell, who had established a character by successful operations in the West, relieved General Hunter, and by his urbanity, and an undefined and indefinable magnetism, had captivated the soldiers, while his reputation as a successful general inspired them with a belief that the department of the South would thereafter have opportunity to make for itself a place in the history of the war, by solid achievements. Poor man! how little he knew of the lack of material, of opportunity and force, in his new command. Better for him had he remained in a subordinate position in the West, where the field was large, and afforded encouragement for the exhibition of military skill and genius.

The work of repairing the fort was carried on energetically, and an occasional excursion up the river, or to neighboring islands, relieved the monotony of garrison duty. One expedition to Bluffton, on the May River, for the purpose of destroying the salt works, resulted not only in its immediate object, but in securing a large supply of excellent and convenient furniture, including a piano for headquarters. The blockade-runner Emma, having for a long time been tied to the wharf at Savannah, made an effort to escape with its cargo of cotton. Just as the sun was beginning to light up the horizon, it was discovered near the entrance to Wright's River, hard and fast, with a receding tide. Boats were manned and sent with all speed to secure her, but too late to save more than the scorched and blackened remains of her valuable cargo of cotton. The fact that an English steamer had, by the contributions of the ladies of Savannah, been converted into a ram of powerful armament kept the garrison on the lookout for an attack, until it became known through deserters that she was an unwieldy mass of iron, with engines of insufficient capacity to move her against the ordinary current of the river.

One morning our gunboats, in the spirit of mere bravado, ran up the river to within range of Fort Jackson and the batteries near, but without result, except to show how poorly both were provided with artillery. Had the navy made a serious attempt on Savannah, we always felt that it would have met with but feeble opposition. There had grown up a wholesome dread of our gunboats, especially of the ironclads, and although our troops met with obstinate resistance, wherever the navy could penetrate the way was almost undisputed.

While affairs were thus comparatively stagnated in the department, Captain Farrell and myself were hard at work recruiting, and, as a result, the regiment was brought up to nearly its original number. It was a pleasant relief from the stale, stupid life in garrison, and afforded an opportunity .to recover from the dreadful effects of the exposure on the swamps and islands of the Savannah. Some of the duties, however, were by no means agreeable; and when the order came for a return to the regiment, it was very welcome. We had been away long enough, and were quite willing that others should take our places; and October 2, when we rejoined the regiment, it was with a feeling of pride that we took up the regular duties of army life again.

During our absence, the officers had been accustomed to meet together to discuss tactics and military law, and it was apparent that we must make special exertion to place ourselves abreast of those who had thus profited: Some few changes had taken place. At night the "All's well," which every hour was carried round the fort from sentinel to sentinel, proclaimed the fact that every one was watchful, and illustrated the system which prevailed. The several expeditions to Bluffton had furnished our quarters with useful and attractive furniture, and, with every convenience for garrison duty, we should have been content, except for the feeling that we might be serving our country better in more active operations.

October 9, General Mitchell and staff visited the fort, and it soon became known that an expedition was planned in which a portion at least of our regiment would take part. From that time until the 21st, the companies which were to join the expedition engaged in target practice every day, and there was much emulation among them. The officers also joined in the practice, for the sake of encouragement. In the meantime the steamboat Planter made another expedition to Bluffton, to complete the demolition of the salt works. Just as we were about to cast off from the dock to return to the fort, the Confederates, who had been awaiting their opportunity, attacked us, and for a few moments the firing was quite sharp. Owing to the low state of the tide, our artillery was useless, until, having cut the hawser, we swung out into the stream, when a few discharges of grape and canister scattered the enemy and we proceeded back to the fort. Our casualties were one killed and several wounded. The frequent expeditions had stripped the town of almost everything portable, and it is not surprising that the inhabitants were desperately angry. It was a pretty village, apparently a summer resort for the wealthier people of Charleston and Savannah. The houses, for the most part of neat and attractive appearance and embowered in trees, stretched along for some distance on the high table-land near the water, and the shore of the river was dotted here and there with boat and bathing houses of pretty design. Deep ravines ran from the river back through the town until lost in the darkened shades of the woods beyond. But the houses were desolate and given up to pillage, the happy households scattered, lost in the whirlpool of mad rebellion, fathers and sons were measuring out their life-blood in the rebel army, and mothers and daughters were mourning over the loss of friends and homes and all that makes life dear, while suffering the terrible privations of an invaded country. A sad picture of the cruelties of war!

CHAPTER IX.

Expedition to Coosawhatchie. Landing at Dawson's plantation. March to Coosawhatchie. Ambuscade. Firing on Confederate train. Confederate prisoners. Destruction of track. Retreat. Peril of Lieutenant Corwin. Lieutenant Blanding wounded. Pocataligo expedition a failure. Perilous voyage back to Pulaski. Confederate weapons. Yellow fever. Death of General Mitchell. His character. Review of Coosawhatchie.

OCTOBER 21 we embarked on the steamer Planter, six companies of fifty men each, and proceeded to Hilton Head, where we joined the main body of troops belonging to the expedition, and, accompanied by a number of gunboats, started for the point of attack. The morning of the 22d found us opposite Mackey's Point on the Coosawhatchie River, in rear of the fleet, which numbered in all fifteen gunboats and transports. This was the point of disembarkation for the main body, but we proceeded farther up the river, accompanied by two gunboats. We had not gone far before our boat grounded on a point on the Dawson plantation near the house, and we landed in small boats. A few cavalry pickets delayed us a little, but we finally started up the road with Company H deployed as skirmishers under command of the writer. This road led directly to the village of Coosawhatchie, and ran nearly parallel to the railroad. The attempt to skirmish through the woods was soon abandoned, owing to the dense growth of plants and shrubs and trailing vines. The Spanish bayonet plant was the most formidable, its thick bristling points presenting such obstacles to our progress that we were soon compelled to confine ourselves to an advanced position on the road. Where other roads intersected, guards were stationed. A short march brought us to an open space, with the railroad in plain sight, only about two hundred yards distant from the turnpike. Without waiting for special orders, Company H was deployed along the railway embankment, at the same time that the whistle of an engine warned us that a train was approaching. Carefully posting the men along the track, but out of sight, a cautious observation discovered the train stopped a short distance below us. It was a period of anxious suspense, until we were assured that it was again in motion, when, the most careful instructions having been given as to when and how to fire, we awaited its approach. Several platform cars were loaded with troops, and as we poured in our fire upon them, at only a few feet distance, the effect was terrible. In an instant those crowded masses of humanity had disappeared. Some were killed and more were wounded, but a large number jumped from the train and concealed themselves in the swamp and woods. A few were taken prisoners, but the wounded were left to be cared for by their own people, who were known to be near by, as we had no means of caring for them. It was a cruel ambuscade, for as they came to the place where we were awaiting them, it was apparent that they had no intimation of our presence in the vicinity. We hoped to injure the engine and so wreck the train, and a number of the most reliable men were assigned to that special duty; but it passed on out of sight, and we gave our attention to the destruction of the railroad, under the direction of the engineers who had accompanied us for such purposes. Not much was accomplished before heavy firing warned us that we could not delay; and, collecting the prisoners and such arms as we had captured, we proceeded to join the regiment. This had arrived at the open space just in season to discharge the little cannon, which the colonel had borrowed from the navy, at the passing train, when it pushed on, hoping to destroy the bridge which crossed the river a little farther up the road; but the Confederates were found strongly entrenched, with heavy batteries guarding its approaches, and, after carefully feeling of the position and drawing the fire of the batteries, the colonel was obliged to give the order to return. Company H was again thrown out as skirmishers, and, discovering what was supposed to be a Confederate detachment, commenced firing. Fortunately, before any injury was done, it was ascertained that it was Lieutenant Corwin with his company, which had been left to guard a threatening point. Nothing further occurred until we reached the boat, when, as we were embarking, the little knot of cavalry which had been closely watching our movements for some time rode rapidly forward and gave us a volley, by which Lieutenant Blanding, of the 3d Rhode Island Artillery, who accompanied us, was severely wounded. A few shells from the little Parrot gun on our bow dispersed them, and we steamed down the river without further casualty. The main body of the expedition had the usual experience at Pocotaligo, where they hoped to be able to effectually destroy the railroad. The force was too small, and was repulsed with severe loss. We nevertheless expected to renew the attempt the next day; but this purpose was given up, and we were ordered back to the fort. The perils of our return passage were quite equal to any that we had encountered, for in the intense darkness the pilot lost his way, and for a long time we were buffeted about by wind and waves, not knowing what was to become of us. The next day we had leisure to examine the weapons we had captured. It was a curious collection, consisting of rifles, swords of venerable age, and a species of cleaver, much resembling those commonly used by butchers, showing to what extremities the Home Guards, at least, were already reduced. As I write I have a specimen of the last mentioned weapon on my table, personally taken from a rebel at Coosawhatchie.

October 28, General Mitchell was reported seriously ill with yellow fever, and General Brannon assumed command of the department.

HEADQUARTERS OF HUNTER AND MITCHELL.

October 29, Dr. Strickland, our chaplain, an old friend of General Mitchell, was sent for to attend him. October 30, General Mitchell died, at 6 P. M. And as others at Hilton Head were prostrated with the same disease, there was danger that it would spread through the department, and every precaution was taken to guard against it. The loss of General Mitchell was a severe blow. He had the confidence of the troops, had shown his ability as a commander, and was supposed to be in such relations with the authorities at Washington as to promise such additions to our forces as would enable us to undertake something of importance. Our last expedition would perhaps have had a better result had he been well enough to assume its direction. As it was, the colors of the Whippy Swamp Guards, with the prisoners and arms, captured by Company H of our regiment, were the only favorable results, while the complete failure of the main expedition, with the loss of so many men, added another to the disheartening blows from which the department had suffered from the beginning. And now the loss of General Mitchell, on whom our hopes were centred, left us without a promise for the future. Soon after our return from Coosawhatchie, two deserters from the 1st Georgia regiment, called the Whippy Swamp Guards, came down from Savannah. They reported the loss of thirty men, their major, and the engineer of the train, at Coosawhatchie, together with their colors. These latter, which we had in our possession, attested the correctness of their statement in at least one particular. Had the Confederates whom we attacked been commanded by any one of ordinary ability, troops would have been sent down by the railroad to cut off our retreat, for there was but one road by which we could return, and this was bordered on either side by impenetrable woods, so that a small force could have held us and made our escape impossible. It is probable that our attack at the railroad so disconcerted them that before they recovered, it was too late to interrupt our rapid retreat. Those who sent us into such a trap either knew nothing of the country, or were willing to make the sacrifice of our command for the sake of drawing off troops from the main point of attack. Looking back upon it now, it seems a part of the blundering operations which characterized our department for the most of the time that we were there, the attack on Pulaski forming a happy exception to the general rule.

CHAPTER X.

At Fort Pulaski. Changes at Dawfuskie. Amusements. The pride and taste of the soldiers in fitting up their quarters. Mosquitoes and other pests. Thanksgiving celebration. Incidents of garrison life. Flag of truce. Confederate ironclad. New Year's Day. Mr. Logan's account of the condition of things in Savannah. Prices of provisions, etc. Resignation and departure of Chaplain Strickland. Inspector-General Townsend's and Colonel Green's opinion of the regiment. Flag of truce. Interesting interview with Adjutant-General Gordon and Lieutenant Styles, of the Confederate army. Formation of negro regiments. Our theatre. Building a steam-launch. Deserters. Capture of blockade-runner. Effect of garrison life on the regiment. Capture of Confederate ironclad Atlanta.

AFTER our return from Coosawhatchie, for a time, we were left undisturbed in garrison. The work of repairing the fort and replacing the guns injured in the bombardment continued, with company and battalion drill, whenever the weather permitted. November 4, a few officers made a trip to Dawfuskie, visiting Munger's and Stoddard's; but neglect and decay were manifest everywhere. A few old negroes, abandoned because of inability to bring further profit, with the desolated homes, together exhibited the barbarisms of war and slavery.

The cold weather soon relieved our apprehensions from yellow fever; and affairs at the fort moved on in the old sluggish current. Games of ball on the terre-plein, and hunting on the islands near, varied the monotony somewhat, and artillery drill added somewhat to our regular duties. The ducks in the bay were numerous; and, as we had collected quite a fleet of boats, parties were made up, almost daily, to hunt them.

Thanksgiving was approaching, and we determined to make the day memorable. The officers contributed liberally, and committees were appointed to plan for a celebration, which should not only afford pleasure to ourselves, but attract to the fort the general officers of the department, as well as others. November 18, we indulged in a regatta. The colonel had selected the most promising craft, and fitted it up quite handsomely; others also had apparently been fortunate in their selections, but Captain Strickland, while obliged to take an inferior boat, had in Company H the most skilful sailors of the regiment, who, for love of their captain and the honor of the company, worked with a will to overcome all inequalities. The trial trip of our boat was made very early in the morning of the day on which the race occurred, and resulted in christening it the "Tub," by those who had watched its movements. A few changes and alterations were made, and it was ready to start with the others. The race was very exciting, and the course a long one, and it was for some time doubtful which would win the prize, but when the Tub came into the dock, having distanced the whole fleet, by common consent she received the more reputable name of Maggie.

During the pleasant days of autumn, scarcely a day passed without some form of amusement or recreation. The Sabbath, while we were in garrison, was usually observed in a becoming manner, and was a day of rest from work and play, save in the matter of inspection. Regularly every Sunday morning the colonel, accompanied by his staff, made a thorough examination of the interior of the fort, and such was the character of the men, and the discipline which prevailed, that no effort was spared to make these inspections satisfactory. The companies which occupied the casemates on two sides of the fort availed themselves of all the materials at hand to fit them up in a manner not only to secure the greatest comfort to themselves, but to render them most attractive in appearance. And it was a great pleasure to note from Sabbath to Sabbath the ingenuity and skill displayed in the arrangements for eating and sleeping, as well as for general effects. Bunks were made, either single or double, and tastefully covered with colored netting, to ward off the attacks of mosquitoes and sand flies. Tables, chairs, and lounges of various designs occupied the spaces around the guns, while dogs, cats, 'coons, and other pets shared the quarters and the messes. The season for sand flies, mosquitoes, and fleas, passed by with the warm weather, but each for a time had proven severe trials to us all. First the sand flies swarmed in countless numbers, microscopic in size, all bite and poison, penetrating everywhere, and, while they lasted, the agony of dress parade, with the men at rest, will be remembered, but cannot be described. The mosquitoes were quite tolerable, but when, under the hot sun of midsummer, the fleas made their appearance, there was little rest night or day. Walking on the shore, it seemed sometimes as if every grain of sand had been quickened into life, like the dragon's teeth of Jason.

Rumors reached us, from time to time, that an effort would be made to recapture the fort, and General Beauregard was reported to have stated, in a speech, that but a few days would elapse before he would replace the present commandant. Others have made similar mistakes, and to few is given the spirit of prophecy.

November 27, Thanksgiving Day, opened bright and beautiful, the atmosphere clear and cool. All preparations had been made, and we awaited the coming of our guests. The chaplain consecrated the day in a short but interesting sermon upon the political aspects of the country. After the discourse, the amusements of the day commenced, with target-shooting and boat-races. When these were concluded, the officers marched to the south dock, to meet the guests. Three boats came, quite loaded with passengers, among them Generals Brannon and Terry. Proceeding to the fort to the sound of music and the firing of salutes which announced the quality of our visitors, the amusements of the day recommenced, with foot-races, followed by hurdle, sack, and wheel-barrow races, greased pole, greased pig, and other games. Perhaps the most ludicrous were the attempts of the negroes, with hands tied behind them, to pick out with their teeth the gold piece concealed in a tub of flour. Finally the day closed with dress parade by the non-commissioned officers and privates, in which the most grotesque costumes were used, and the largest liberty permitted. Taking advantage of this, the peculiarities of the officers were brought out with the grossest exaggerations, manner and tone being imitated so well, and withal in such good-natured frolicsome spirit, that the subjects of the pleasantries enjoyed it equally with the others. The published orders were admirable hits, ending with the one attributed to Major Beard, which, after announcing the death of a member of the regiment, concluded with, "The God of battles will give him a soldier's rest by order of O. T. Beard, Major

Commanding." A long nooning gave ample time for the dinner, which was spread in a temporary building on the terre-plein, and consisted of a variety of fish, fowl, and joints, with the usual accompaniments. The evening and most of the night were given up to dancing. At midnight a supper was served, and many of us retired, but a few, who had passed the bounds of moderation in their libations, served to keep alive the echoes of song and laughter until the morning brought exhaustion, and permitted a little rest. The day was a memorable one, contrasting as it did so severely with the events which placed us there and continued to disturb the country. The following day we parted with our guests, and resumed the old routine.

At this time our company was stationed on Tybee Island, with headquarters in the Martello Tower, and it was a common trip to run over and dine with Swartwout, who was one of the most genial and hospitable officers in the regiment. He had very comfortable apartments on the top of the tower, and his men were pleasantly disposed in neat and cheerful barracks near by. There were horses to ride, and a long, beautiful, and solid beach to ride on, little to do, no special annoyances, plenty of game and an almost independent command, so that those detailed there were inclined to remain.

Soon after our arrival at the fort for garrison duty, a bed of fine large and luscious oysters was discovered near by, having been planted by the former occupants of the fort, by whose labors we profited much, for the supply seemed unlimited. Base-ball became a regular institution, in which the whole garrison joined, from the colonel down. When the officers were not playing, the men occupied the ground, when off duty. And it was well, for we needed all the exercise we could get, on account of the enervating effect of the long

MARTELLO TOWER, TYBEE ISLAND.

confinement in the fort, and we wished to be ready for active service, which we trusted would come in time.

December 24, Colonel Barton returned from Hilton Head with the announcement that Lieutenant-Colonel Beard had resigned, and his resignation had been accepted, and that several ironclads were expected from the North.

December 27, the steamboat Mattano conveyed a party up the river on flag of truce. Starting early in the forenoon, we proceeded slowly to a point nearly opposite St. Augustine's Creek, when we were hailed by the officer of a Confederate picket, and, having dropped anchor, awaited the return of the messenger which had been sent to the ram Georgia as soon as we appeared in sight. This was plainly visible, about a mile distant, — a low, sullen mass of iron, apparently immovable. While waiting the return of the messenger, we had ample opportunity to examine it, but could make out little beyond her general shape. Designed to clear the river and vicinity of our gunboats, she had thus far proved a failure, and, as confessed by an officer who visited us, had greatly disappointed those who had furnished the means to build her. The officer sent to communicate with us was Lieutenant Johnson, who, in the course of a very pleasant conversation, stated that for seventeen years he was in the United States service. That at the time of our attack on Port Royal he was in command of one of the steamers of Commodore Tatnall's fleet, which was nearly blown out of water by one of our eleven-inch shells. In the afternoon, Captain Sawyer, of General Mercer's staff, came alongside, having started for Pulaski on flag of truce. His boat was manned by sailors from New York.

January 1, 1863, opened with a clear sky and an invigorating atmosphere. It was observed as a holiday, and Captain Elfwing, who could not forget, even in our unfavorable conditions, the good old custom of open house and spread table, invited his friends to partake of his hospitalities. Lieutenant Wallace, who had resigned, spent the day in taking leave of his companions.

January 3, nine men from the 47th New

York State Volunteers, a regiment with which we had been brigaded from the first, and between which and our regiment there had always existed a special friendship, came to the fort in the steamer Mattano, for a match game of of base-ball with our picked nine. They took their defeat in the best humor, and nothing occurred to mar the good-fellowship between the two regiments.

January 8, Mr. Logan, who went up to Savannah December 27, returned to the fort with several ladies. Lieutenant Johnson came with them, and our acquaintance was renewed. Papers were exchanged, and from the Savannah News we gained information which silenced certain unfavorable rumors which had been current in the garrison for some days. Mr. Logan gave an interesting account of what he saw within the Confederate lines, and we note a few of his statements. The supply of clothing had become so reduced that the cast-off garments of past generations were drawn upon, so that the grotesqueness of costumes, even among the better classes, was often ludicrous. The prices of nearly everything had advanced to enormous figures. The following will serve as examples. Tea was fourteen dollars a pound, salt fifteen dollars a bushel, flour from thirty to fifty dollars a barrel, men's boots from twenty to forty dollars per pair. He further stated that his brother-in-law paid a hundred dollars for a coat made of Kentucky jean, and fifty dollars for two pairs of hand cards for carding cotton. He himself paid two dollars for a tooth-brush, and four dollars for a daguerreotype. Sugar was sold for seventy-five cents per pound by the hogshead, and other articles in proportion. Merchants had but little in their stores; and great inconvenience, and even suffering, generally prevailed. From these facts we derived great encouragement. If they indicated the condition of things generally in the South, the war could not last long. The report of the capture of Vicksburg, about this time, strengthened this feeling. The news, generally, was encouraging.

February 3, Generals Hunter, Foster, Negley, Potter, and Seymour visited the fort. General Hunter was quite extravagant in his praises of the regiments. February 6, Dr.

Strickland left us, and was not expected to return. He was an excellent chaplain. Faithful, earnest, and fearless, he helped materially in keeping the regiment to its high standard of morals and propriety. While not aggressive, he was constant in his labors, and was heartily respected in them. There was a wholesome and agreeable freedom in his manner, combined with dignity of habit and speech, which we liked. He had many warm friends, and, if any enemies, they were not known.

February 9, the regiment was inspected by Colonel Green, the assistant inspector-general of the army, who came to the fort accompanied by General E. D. Townsend, Adjutant-General, U. S. A. They both expressed themselves very much pleased at our appearance, and complimented us very highly.

February 16, I was despatched on another flag of truce, with Captain Kenzie, of General Hunter's staff, who was entrusted with special business for headquarters. Near Bird Island, the steamboat Ida met us, and Captain Gordon, adjutant-general of General Mercer's staff, with wife and two children, came on board our boat, accompanied by Captain and Lieutenant Styles of the Virginia army. They were all people of education and refinement, and during the several hours that we spent together, there was no suggestion of personal antagonism as an outgrowth of the general attitude which we maintained towards each other. In spite of my earnest protest against the introduction of any irritating subject, the war, its causes, and its different phases, were discussed with freedom, but without the least appearance of bitterness. Mrs. Gordon and family had suffered privations in common with others, and Lieutenant Styles spoke of the division of the army to which he was attached as often without shoes, and even sufficient food, but bearing everything without complaint. The coat he had on, made of ordinary gray cloth, cost one hundred and fifty dollars, and he had ordered a pair of cavalry boots, to cost sixty dollars — thus corroborating the statements of Mr. Logan. The picture which he drew of the soldiers of the Confederate army, — marching over the snow without shoes, with a cake of gingerbread in hand, costing a dollar, and a newspaper in pocket, costing twenty-five cents, — would have been pathetic had it not suggested such a lamentable want of judgment, in preferring the luxury of gingerbread and newspapers to the comfort and protection of suitable covering for the feet. We parted with mutual expressions of personal esteem, knowing that within the hour of our parting, we might be called upon, in the discharge of duty to which we were bound, to take each other's life, while we equally lamented the necessity for such brutality.

February 20, reports reached us of difficulty between General Hunter and some of the officers on the staffs of the new generals who had come to the department from North Carolina, who showed too little respect for the negro soldiers, the pets of the commanding general. And this reminds me of neglect in overlooking the fact that, in the formation of the negro regiments, Lieutenant Corwin obtained the position of major, and several of our sergeants and corporals obtained commissions. Advanced positions in these regiments were offered to several of our officers, who declined to accept them.

February 23, our theatre was opened, with the following entertainment: — Address by Corporal Michaels. Singing by the members. Farce, "Family Jars." Song, "The Flea," by Owens, of Company H. Recitation by Hutchinson. Light balancing by Dr. Haven. Tragedy, 1st act of "Richard III." Song by Dickson. Concluding with the tableau, "Washington's Grave." The theatre was very pretty, and the performances excellent. The scene-painting was done by Harrison, who was by profession a scenic artist, and was very good. From this time forward, during our stay at the fort, performances were continued regularly, and afforded a great deal of pleasure.

March 3, several officers went to the Ogeechee river to witness the attack on Fort McAllister by the ironclads. About this time a little engine and boiler were completed, under the direction of Captain Paxson, out of materials found in the fort, and placed in a large boat, which had floated down to the island. They worked satisfactorily, and this little craft was used for a long time in trips about the island and to neighboring points. Our regiment might be taken as an example of the material of our army. Every profession, and almost every department of mechanical pursuits, was represented, and, whatever work was required, there was no lack of such as were familiar with it.

March 15, four men, comprising a Confederate picket, came in to the fort, bringing their officer with them, much against his will. They were well armed, with Maynard rifles and Colt's revolvers. In all, twelve deserters came in within ten days. Day after day we were called upon to entertain visitors, and the fort became a place of resort for the idle and curious in the department. The theatre was a great attraction.

March 30, a small schooner was discovered near the entrance to Munger's River, and the colonel started for her in the Mattano. At first she hoisted the English colors, but was compelled to acknowledge that she was a blockade-runner, bound for Savannah with a load of salt. She was our first prize.

March 31, we learned, through Mr. Whitney, the designer of the monitor Keokuk, who was

NEW IRONSIDES AND MONITORS.

visiting his cousin, Captain Lockwood, that there were now eight ironclads at Hilton Head, or near Charleston Harbor, which meant that something was to be done. The men were soon set to work moving mortars to the south dock for shipment. Great activity prevailed; constant communication was kept up with Hilton Head by signal to Braddock's Point; and a steamboat was nearly all the time at the service of Colonel Barton. In addition to our regiment, a company of the 3d Rhode Island Artillery, under Captain Gould, had for a long time, formed a part of the garrison; and at this time several gunboats were in the river, to help protect the fort against any attack which might be made on Pulaski while our ironclads were operating against the forts in Charleston Harbor.

April 7, an attack was made upon Fort Sumter, which was unsuccessful, owing to the obstructions in the channel, which confined the operations of our fleet. The Keokuk, which took the most advanced position, and received the heaviest fire, was so injured that she sank on the following morning.

From this time until June 3 nothing occurred of special interest. We all had leisure for recreation, which was really needed to overcome the effect of confinement in this debilitating climate. Every fair day, after the regular drills, the terre-plein was turned into a playground. Every one drifted into habits of idleness, and while an admirable opportunity was afforded, during our stay in the fort, for reading and study, few had the inclination to engage in serious or profitable pursuits; and so many were inclined to occupations of a frivolous and demoralizing character that it is safe to say that the morals of the regiment suffered a severer strain during our stay in Fort Pulaski than during all the remainder of its service in the army.

June 3, several companies were ordered to be ready with cooked rations, and it soon became known that Bluffton was to be burned. Why this order was issued, we never knew; but it was carried out most literally. Judging from the force detailed, opposition must have been expected; but the work was accomplished without any hindrance, and the beau-

THE INTERIOR OF FORT SUMTER.

tiful little village was reduced to a mass of ruins.

June 12, General Hunter was relieved by General Quincy A. Gilmore, the same who was captain of engineers in the first expedition to Port Royal.

June 17, we became aware that something unusual was taking place in Warsaw Sound; and after an early breakfast, several of us took positions favorable for observation, on that portion of the ramparts overlooking that quarter. A number of steamers were visible, and for a few moments there was heavy firing. We thought we distinguished the rebel ironclad Atlanta, formerly the Frugal, and the return of the steamboat Island City from the scene of operations confirmed this impression. From her we received a full account of the affair. The Atlanta came down Wilmington River, expecting to capture the two ironclads, who were on the lookout for her, but four shots from the Nahant were all that was needed to crush in her sides, and reduce her to submission. At close range, even her four inches of iron plate, backed by fifteen inches of solid oak, were not proof against the heavy guns of the monitor. The other vessels which came down from Savannah to see and perhaps participate somewhat in the fight did not wait for their share, but returned with all speed to report the sad failure.

CHAPTER XI.

Good-by to Fort Pulaski. At St. Helena Island, under General Strong. Billinghurst and Regua battery. Folly Island. Masked batteries. Attack on Morris Island. Killed and wounded of the regiment. Captain Lent. Capture of Confederate batteries. Building batteries. Hot work and little rest. Completion of batteries. Assault on Wagner. Badly managed. Terrible losses. General Strong. Negro soldiers. Their effect upon the Confederates. After the assault. The shelling by the Confederates. Incident.

JUNE 18, General Gilmore arrived at the fort, and in the evening a telegraphic despatch was received,— for, some time before this, a telegraphic cable had been successfully laid between Braddock's Point and the fort,-- ordering us to have eight companies ready to start in the morning, with cooked rations. Although we were ready at the time appointed, it was decided to be better to defer embarkation until evening, that it might not become known to the Confederates that the garrison was so weakened. Accordingly, when the darkness of night had settled down on the fort, the eight companies marched to the dock and embarked in the Ben De Ford, which steamed away from the fort, but anchored off Tybee Island for the night. Companies G and I were left behind; but before we started, the officers all gathered together, and joined in "Auld Lang Syne." Seldom had such a solemn feeling rested upon us, and the cheers and good-wishes of those who parted there were to many the last words of fellowship together upon earth.

The following morning, we passed the Atlanta, on our way to St. Helena Island. It was a formidable-looking craft, being supplied with a heavy armament, and all the appliances for offence and defence, including an immense ram and an ingenious contrivance for exploding torpedoes. Arrived at St. Helena Island, our destination, we found ourselves in the brigade of General Strong.

June 27, the writer was placed in command of the Billinghurst and Regua battery, and separated from the regiment. As soon as detailed, reported to General Strong, and had twenty-five men detailed from the several regiments of the brigade to handle the pieces.

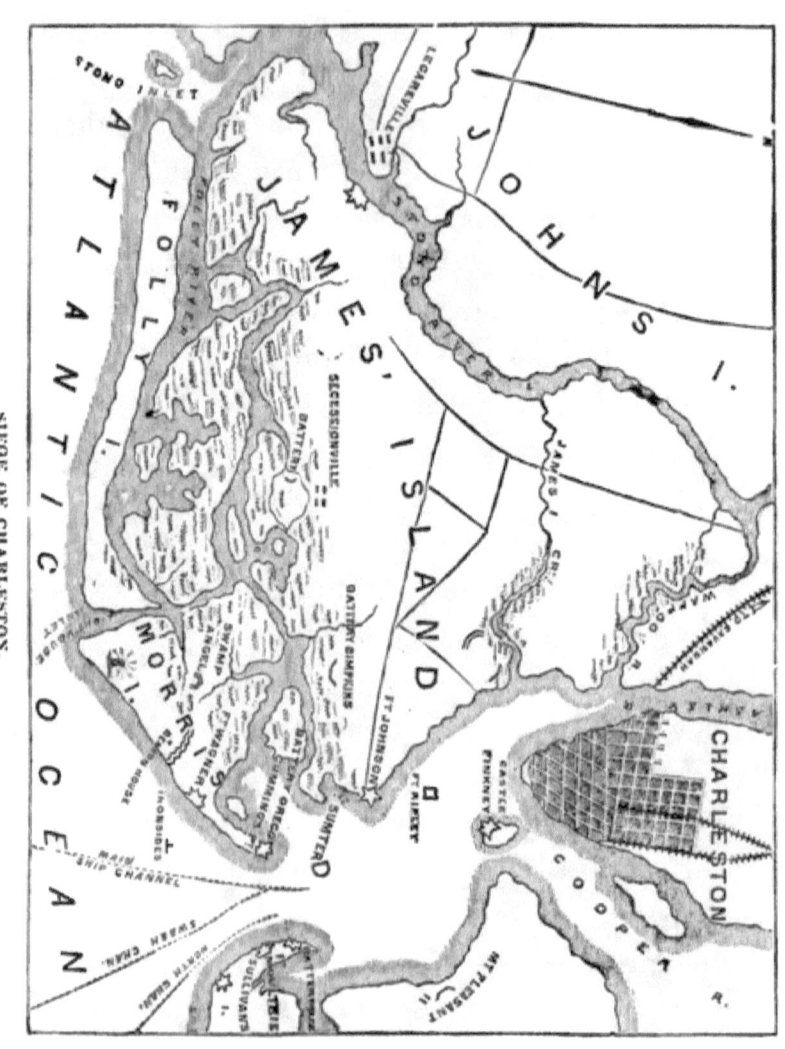

SIEGE OF CHARLESTON.

Each of these consisted of twenty-five rifle barrels on a carriage, so arranged that the fire from a single cap, opposite the centre barrel, was through a tube communicated to all, so that they could be discharged simultaneously. The barrels were heavy, with long range, and, as a defence against attack of infantry, might be very effective. The idea was similar to the French mitrailleuse; but whether borrowed from it, we cannot tell. This was the only battery of the kind ever used in the department, and, being entirely new, every moment was occupied in practice, in getting the range, and in securing the necessary equipments. Worse than all, it was necessary to improvise a drill while the practice was going on, but General Strong, who was one of the noblest, kindest, and most considerate of men, assisted in every way, and by all the means at his command. It was not long before we were as much captivated by his military bearing and his gentle urbanity of manner as the other officers and men of his brigade. It is given to but few men to attach others to them as he did.

July 4, we were ordered on board the Harriet M. Weed, and proceeded to Folly Island, on the northerly portion of which we encamped until the 10th, when we moved up to the other end of the island, in rear of our batteries. These contained about fifty guns, and had been masked by a grove of trees until this morning, when a clearing had been made, and the guns opened fire. Only the day previous, a number of Confederate officers had been out on the sand-bar which at low tide almost connected Folly with Morris Island, and made a careful inspection of the vicinity, with their field-glasses, all the time in plain sight of our men behind the batteries, but without discovering anything. The bombardment was a disagreeable surprise to them. Arrived behind the batteries, we were compelled to go their whole length and return, on account of confusion of orders, while the shot and shell from the Confederate batteries opposite played around us in the most reckless manner.

That night we crossed to Morris Island, and encamped on the beach. In the meantime the 48th, with other troops, had been massed near the end of Folly Island, and as soon as the cannonading from our guns ceased, landed on Morris Island, charged the Confederate works, and, proceeding on, cleared every obstruction, even to the very foot of Wagner. But not without loss. Quite a number were killed and wounded. Among the killed was Captain Lent of Company A, a man of genial, happy disposition, beloved by every one. Although a brave, earnest, and competent officer, he was so quiet and retiring in his habits that he seemed almost out of place in such scenes, and it was hard to reconcile so gentle and amiable a life with such a sudden and cruel death. While encamped on Folly Island, he called at the battery on his way to the front, and I well remember his expression as we parted: "How I wish I had your place! I would rather have it than the command of the regiment." It was not of danger that he thought, but of the independence of the command. Before the attack, our regiment was divided for convenience of landing, and while our guns were thundering against the batteries opposite, the men were waiting in anxious expectancy; and when the word was given they shot across the little strip of water, and, in the face of a murderous fire, rushed up the beach, and with fixed bayonets carried all before them. There was no faltering, but only an onward movement; and, although many fell, others supplied their places, and with cheer upon cheer they cleared the Confederate works, capturing men, guns, camp-equipage, and everything, until the recall was sounded, and they came slowly back to count their dead and wounded. It was a gallant charge, and in it General Strong set the example, when, leaving shoes in the clinging sand, he rushed forward, the first to land, and the last to realize the necessity for a recall. It was a glorious charge and a glorious success, which gave a vantage-ground for our troops on which to plant their batteries, and a place for successful operations against the strong defences of Charleston. Had the proper use been made of this early success, Wagner would have been ours; but, unfortunately, the attack on this fort was delayed until the following morning, when, with a garrison re-enforced, our attacking column was easily repulsed. The days that followed were full of labor and exposure. The guns of Wagner and

NOISELESS HAULING OF THE GUNS.

Sumter searched every nook and cranny of the island, and many men lay down at night to sleep, to waken in the Eternal City. As fast as possible, guns were hurried up into position to bear upon Wagner, and the heavy armaments of the ironclads kept up a constant clamor, but with little effect; shot and shell came flying

BOMB AND SPLINTER PROOF.

into camp in all directions. General Strong's headquarters were fairly uprooted by a bursting shell, and when solicited to move to a less exposed position he laughed, as if it were only play. Hour by hour he grew into the affections of his command, and it is certain that no officer was ever more beloved. After a time, earthworks were thrown up across the island, near Wagner; and the men, from habit, learned to protect themselves in some measure from the enemy's fire. July 13, the 48th were at the front for twenty-four hours, during which time the Confederates made a sortie, but were repulsed with considerable loss. A sergeant endeavored to capture Lieutenant Tantum, but made a bad mistake. The powerful grasp of

FORT WAGNER AT POINT OF ASSAULT.

the lieutenant was not to be resisted, and the sergeant went to the rear, an humble prisoner. Attached to our battery, and under my command, was a small company of sharpshooters, with telescopic rifles, who buried themselves in the sand close to the walls of Wagner in the hour before light in the morning, and proved most effective in controlling the fire of the fort. Not a head or hand could appear without being reminded of their presence.

July 18, the attack on Fort Wagner commenced at about 10 A. M., and a steady fire from our batteries and the ironclads was kept up until evening. The following is the account of the assault, written by J. A. Barrett, who was second lieutenant of Company H: —

"We lay on our arms all day, and just before dark were formed in column by companies, and advanced under a galling fire up the beach. It was a trying hour, our ranks thinning at every step. For much of the way the right of our column was obliged to wade in the water. On our left another column composed of the 54th Massachusetts colored regiment, under Colonel Shaw, also advanced on the fort. We waded the moat and scaled the parapet. Our loss was terrible, sometimes whole companies being mowed down at once. We jumped over the parapet into one bastion where there were two guns, but the firing was so hot that we were unable to turn them to any use. Darkness was upon us, and we could see nothing. The supporting columns coming up in our rear, poured in a heavy fire, mistaking us for the rebels. Our killed and wounded kept piling up. A rebel officer for some purpose came among our men, and was seized by a private of the 48th, who called to Colonel Barton that he had a prisoner. To which the colonel replied: 'Take him to the rear.' 'But he won't come,' said the private, who was nicknamed 'Plucky.' 'If he wont yield, then bayonet him,' was the order; when a wounded man dragged himself up, and, with all his remaining strength, plunged his bayonet into the side of the rebel officer, and, falling back, expired. A retreat was ordered, but was not altogether understood, and some fifty of our men remained and continued firing. I was severely wounded in the thigh, but roused myself, and directed the fire of these few men as best I could, collecting ammunition from the dead and wounded. When this gave out, I ordered all who could to go to the rear. This section of the fort was literally full of dead and wounded, piled up even with the parapet. I crossed over their bodies, slid down the slope and crossed the moat, which was full of our dead. A rebel sentry was pacing up and down the beach, but by keeping near the bank I was able to pass him. My scabbard was shot away, my pistol bent and useless, and, leaning on my sword, I hobbled down the beach to camp. The 48th went into this assault with five hundred men and sixteen officers, and three hundred men and fourteen officers were killed, wounded, or prisoners."

While this brief account is valuable, as the statement of a cool, self-possessed, and brave officer, who participated in the assault, and was an eye-witness to what he states, no words can adequately describe the horrors of that night. Sufficient time had elapsed, since the occupation of the island by our troops, to allow of a complete and careful preparation for the assault, which the enemy had reason to expect. A large re-enforcement was added to the garrison, and the men were most carefully drilled in the minutest details, to provide against every possible emergency. The heavy bombardment which preceded the assault, while it seemed as if it would tear the fort from its foundation, had really no serious effect in weakening it; and as soon as it ceased, the men were withdrawn from the bombproofs, where they had been completely protected, and assigned to their positions, and, when our troops made the assault, were as ready to receive them as if not

FORT WAGNER, SEA FRONT.

a cannon had been fired. On our part, there seemed to be a want of accurate information, and of carefully matured plan, which resulted in confusion of action; while on their part, there was the most intelligent and thorough preparation possible, and most perfect concert of action between all those assigned to special duties in the defence. The result was inevitable, and the carnage terrible. The responsibility of the assault was generally ascribed to General Seymour, and, as subsequent events clearly proved, it was a useless sacrifice of life. General Gilmore continued to plant batteries, by which we not only reached the forts in the vicinity, but, with the famous Swamp Angel guns, threw shot and shell a distance of five miles into the city of Charleston. These batteries, and the mine which he constructed, which destroyed one whole force of Wagner, compelled its evacuation on the night of September 6.

On the night of the assault, July 18, there was no sleep in the 48th. It was past midnight when the last of the men came in from the fort, and the horrible scenes through which they had passed, and the anguish of grief over friends and comrades, maimed and wounded, or lying silent in that pit of darkness and blood, forbade all thought of rest. Colonel Barton was wounded through the thigh, Lieutenant-Colonel Green, Captains Farrell and Hurst, and Lieutenant Edwards were dead, and Captain Paxson was mortally wounded. Captains Lockwood, Elfwing, and Swartwout, and Lieutenants Miller, Barrett, and Acker, were also severely wounded. It was a heart-rending sight when, on the following morning, I visited them in the steamer which was to convey them to Hilton Head. No one could doubt the quality of the 48th now. The heroism of the men was only equalled by that of their officers. None

THE SWAMP ANGEL BATTERY.

could have been braver. All the wounded officers had made their escape with the exception of Lieutenants Taylor and Fox, who were left in the hands of the Confederates. While we mourned for our immediate friends and associates, we did not forget that our brigade commander, General Strong, was among the fatally wounded. I had been accustomed to report to him in person for commands for the battery; and, of all the men I have ever known, few have left such deep and such pleasant impressions on my memory as he — of the gentlest and most winning manners, yet always the thorough soldier, brave even to rashness, kind, courteous, and considerate, he grew more and more beloved as he became better known. He never asked men to go where he would not lead the way.

On the night of the assault, my battery was stationed at the outer lines of our defences, on the shore, to resist any counter attack which the Confederates might make, and I witnessed much of its horrors. As one after another of the wounded came in, eager and anxious were the questions asked, until the return of the torn and broken remnants of the proud columns which a few moments before had rushed to victory told too plainly the story of savage butchery and defeat. Well do I remember the appearance of the negro soldiers as they came straggling back from the front that night, for I was not favorably impressed by their conduct.

I have often thought that their presence in the attacking column was a mistake, and that the hatred and disgust which they caused in the minds of the Confederates overcame every other feeling, to such an extent that the instinct of self-defence was converted into brutal ferocity, as was manifest in their treatment not only of the colored soldiers themselves, but the gallant officers who led them. With the highest respect for the opinions of those who have testified to the discipline and valor of the negro troops, I am impelled to say, in spite of the criticisms that my statement may provoke, that my own observation and experience, as well as the experience of others, have convinced me that the prevailing opinion, especially in New England, of the valuable services rendered by colored troops in actual conflict, is erroneous, and that their most effective work during the war was done with the pick and spade. If quickness of perception and independence of thought and action are desirable qualities in a soldier, this conclusion seems both obvious and necessary. After the repulse of the 18th, the Billinghurst and Regua battery was kept at the front all the time, and, although protected somewhat by earthworks, there was no complete guard against the shells which night and day exploded all about us. One of my men was sitting in the sand just outside the battery, when a shell from Wagner literally ploughed him out of his seat. Fortunately, it did not explode, and he only experienced a good shaking-up. Night after night we were obliged to keep watch of those magnificent streams of light which, proceeding from the mortars at Castle Pinkney, seemed charged with intelligence as well as powder, for as they moved through the air and reached the point over our batteries, they appeared to poise themselves as if to select the most vulnerable point, when they descended with a peculiar whizzing sound into our very midst. Our only recourse was, by determining on which side the earthworks they would fall, to make the most expeditious movement to the other side, to await the explosion.

I remember one night when it was determined to plant a *chevaux-de-frise* from our battery to low-water mark. A night was chosen when it was thought that the heavy clouds would obscure the moon and conceal our operations. The wagons proceeded up the beach with the materials, until they had nearly reached the point selected, when the opening clouds disclosed them to the garrison of Wagner. No time was lost in opening upon them with their Armstrong guns, from the parapet. The first shot produced a stampede, and in an instant the teams had turned about, and the horses were scampering back, with the shot and shell skipping about them in the most unceremonious fashion. The sight was so ludicrous that I was thrown off my guard, and exploding with laughter, until the danger of my own position was recalled by the bursting of shells about my head.

CHAPTER XII.

Back to the regiment. Off for St. Augustine. The duties of provost-marshal. The quaint old city. Its pleasant people. Two months of rest. Lieutenant Ingraham. Back to Hilton Head. The regiment reunited. Visit to Morris Island. Captain Eaton. Fort Wagner and its reminders. Lieutenant-Colonel Green.

JULY 30, at my own request, I was relieved from the command of the Billinghurst and Regua battery, and returned to the regiment. While an independent position, it was one in which there was no promise of important service, and I have never heard that the batteries were ever successfully used. They lacked the strength of the ordinary battery, and the mobility of columns of troops. I joined the regiment at Hilton Head just in season to superintend its embarkation for St. Augustine, Major Strickland and Captain Coan being ill.

Arrived at St. Augustine August 2, and remained until October 3. Our duties were light, and opportunity was afforded for recovery from the effects of the Morris Island campaign. As provost-marshal, I had the complete supervision of the city, the receiving of flags of truce, and the regulation and examination of the correspondence between the inhabitants and their friends within the Confederate lines. All fire-arms had been taken from the citizens by my predecessor; but the owners were permitted to use them occasionally for hunting, under certain restrictions. People were allowed to come in and go out of the city, when it was apparent that no harm could result, and the planters outside were encouraged to bring in produce and other supplies under the scrutiny of men detailed for the purpose. The materials of the theatre were brought from Fort Pulaski, and the performances afforded much amusement, and helped to make the regiment popular during our stay. We found many pleasant people, some of whom had never sympathized with the rebellion, and were glad of the protection of United States troops. Others, while bitter and hostile, were incapable of any harm. The quaint old town was in itself a never-ending fund of enjoyment and interest. The men were comfortably quartered, and the officers indulged in unusual luxuries. Among those whom I recall of the good people who resided there were Mrs. Anderson and her son, the doctor, whose delightful home in the suburbs, in its surroundings and furnishing, but more especially in its charming atmosphere of culture and refinement, so often helped us to throw off the hardening and brutalizing effects of army life and associations. The Misses Mather and Perritt, with whom a number of our officers boarded, natives of the North, driven to this softer climate by delicate health, were in the fullest sympathy and accord with us, and were not only exceedingly kind, but afforded much assistance, by reason of their familiar acquaintance with the city, its affairs, and its people.

The two months spent in St. Augustine passed quickly and pleasantly. Occasionally, the pickets were fired upon, but no regular attack was made. Communication was undoubtedly kept up between the citizens and the enemy, outside the city, in spite of the great precautions taken to prevent it. Applicants for admission to the city were reported waiting at the picket stations almost daily, some of whom were received and others turned away. Visitors came to the city by almost every steamer, and the abundant leisure of most of the officers allowed of their generous entertainment. From my office I looked across the square, past the old building with open front, formerly used as a slave mart but now converted into a general market, to the office of the commissary — Lieutenant Ingraham; and frequently, when the duties of the forenoon were well over, we signalled to each other to drop work, and engaged in some form of recreation together. During our stay at St. Augustine we were thrown much together, and the pleasant feelings which I had always entertained towards him ripened into a strong attachment. I think of him now with feelings of peculiar sadness. Some time before the battle of Cold Harbor, his promotion rendered it necessary that he should take his place as an officer of the company to which he was attached. Previous to this he had always been detailed in the quartermaster's or commissary departments. At that battle, while we occupied the Confederate line of works which we had just captured, we were subjected to a merciless enfilading fire, which we could neither avoid nor return effectively. Lieutenant Ingraham, in command of his company, had pressed to the very front, and, while encouraging his men by word and example, he suddenly dropped from my side, and I never saw him more. With a great rush, the enemy was upon us both in front and flank, and we were pushed through the woods, and our wounded and dead were left to their care. Ingraham was a good soldier, a good friend, and a good man. October 3, a steamer, containing the 24th Massachusetts regiment arrived at the dock, and we were ordered to prepare for our departure. October 6, we bade good-by to the old city, to the many good people who had done so much to make our stay among them contented and restful, and to the peculiar comforts and pleasures, which, to so many, were the only suggestion of home that came into their lives during their long term of service. On the 7th we reached Beaufort, S. C., and reported to General Saxton. The next day the writer was ordered by the colonel to proceed with four companies to Seabrook Landing, to guard the shipping. This point was rather an important one at the time, being used as a coaling station and for naval repairs. November 9, one hundred and fifty-six conscripts arrived from New York and were distributed to the various companies of the regiment. November 13, companies G and I, so long detached as garrison of Fort Pulaski, joined us at Hilton Head, where regimental headquarters were then established. November 20, the subject of re-enlistment as veterans began to be agitated, and the promise of thirty days furlough and a bounty were strong inducements. November 25, having business at Morris Island, I took occasion to visit Fort Wagner, which had been rebuilt under the supervision of Captain Eaton of the New York Engineer regiment, a most excellent officer, who seemed almost to belong to us, having had charge of the repairing of Fort Pulaski while we were there as garrison. With him I wandered about the fort, and around the localities marked by special events connected with the siege and assault. But memory was too busy with painful scenes to permit of much satisfaction. As we talked together of old times, and recalled the names of those with whom we had been intimate at Pulaski, it seemed impossible to realize that the clean white sand on which we were then treading had drank in the life-blood of so many, and the clear, bright, sparkling water, that idly played upon the beach, had reached out its eager tongue to lick up the cruel stains. The air was mild, not a cloud obscured the sun's rays, and the silence that reigned about us was profound, almost oppressive, but, as we recalled the past, the din of battle rang in our ears; the flash of musketry pierced through the darkness of night and lighted up a scene of carnage; the groans and cries of the wounded and dying mingled with the shouts and yells and fierce oaths of combatants. The spirit of peace rested upon the landscape which lay spread out before us, and upon the face of the quiet waters which, with gentle embrace, pressed lightly against the shore; but the past came back to us like a mighty surging torrent; a tempest raged; darkness and horror enveloped us, and we turned away. We could not endure it, and were glad to get back to camp, to lose the thought of the past in the performance of present duty.

During this visit, as we talked together of the friends who had fallen, one name more than any other occupied our thoughts and conversation. It was that of Lieutenant-Colonel Green, whom Captain Eaton had known quite intimately when he was quartered with us at Fort Pulaski. Like those of us who had known him longer, he had not only formed a strong personal attachment for him, but, from the peculiar and somewhat opposite traits of character which he exhibited, had become specially interested in watching his career. It was not singular, for no one could be associated with him, for any length of time, without being attracted towards him and becoming interested in him. Possessed of a frank and generous disposition, he was not only beloved by those under him, because of his thoughtful consideration of them, but equally by his fellow-officers, because of his sprightly, sunny temperament. He was welcome everywhere, and, on all social occasions, his quick and susceptible nature caught and communicated the spirit of humor that prevailed, until no one could withstand its influence. He bubbled over with mirth whenever the occasion or surroundings stirred the humorous vein within him, and was the frequent instigator of the harmless practical jokes with which the officers sometimes sought to enliven the dulness of garrison life. I can see him now, as, after a period of duty, he starts out from his quarters in search of recreation, the very personification of mischief. He never needed to go far, for every latch-string was out for him, and none but the hardest and most obdurate could withstand the appeal of his merry eyes and bright, cheery countenance. He was a good soldier, always ready for duty, and in its discharge both earnest and exact. From "grave to gay" was sometimes a rapid transition with him; but he saw every duty to its ending, and, especially when hardship and danger were involved, every fibre of his mental and physical nature was absorbed in its performance. Few will be remembered longer by his comrades than he, and none with more general warmth of affection.

CHAPTER XIII.

Relations between the 47th and 48th regiments. Re-enlistment of veterans. Court-martial. Departure of veterans on furlough. Expedition to Florida. Battle of Olustee. A great blunder. Heavy losses. Admirable conduct of the troops. Dr. Defendorf. The retreat. Return of veterans. Sergeant Thompson. At Palatka. Expedition into the country. Dunn's Creek. Its marvellous beauty. Ludicrous scenes. Good-by to Palatka. At Gloucester Point, Va. A happy change. Shelter tents. General Grant. Army of the James under Butler. General Terry.

OF the several months that followed, until January 31, 1864, little can be gathered from the journals which furnish the materials for this history. Aside from the usual routine of duties incident to life in camp, a few changes took place in the distribution of the companies to the outposts within the district. On Thanksgiving Day the members of the 47th New York State Volunteers were our guests, and on Christmas we partook of their hospitalities, cementing by these courtesies that bond of union between the two regiments which was unbroken during our term of service, and was one of the pleasantest facts in our army experience. The rivalry between the two regiments seemed to manifest itself only in generous expressions and friendly offices.

During this period, the officers used all their influence to induce re-enlistments as veterans, and, as a result, some three hundred or more of the best men in the regiment signified their willingness to sacrifice anew their comfort and safety, their prospects in life, and life itself, if necessary, in the service of their country, if perchance, by such a sacrifice the blessings which they and their fathers had enjoyed, and by which the world had so largely benefited, might be transmitted to future generations. If, after the lapse of years, and in the dim light of the past, such a sacrifice seems a common thing to those who, in security and comfort, at this time, thought of little but of the opportunity afforded, through the waste and destruction of war, for the accumulation of riches, or to those who, too young to take interest in the events of which we write, know nothing of them except as a part of the history of days gone by; it was not a common thing to those who, having already given of the best of their years, and the freshness and vigor of their strength, declared their willingness to plunge anew into those scenes the effect of which they knew full well was to harden their natures, blunt and benumb their sensibilities, and paralyze those finer instincts through which come the enjoyments most prized in life; it was not a common sacrifice for these men to turn again from the sweet influences and tender affections of home and friends that others might be benefited. Nor let it be said that the considerations to which I have referred could have entered the minds of only the intelligent few, while to the great body of the army they were far beyond their thought; for, while we must admit that there were different degrees of intelligence, and that that which formulated itself in clear, distinct, and logical following in some minds was but faintly outlined in others, who so dull that, from the lessons of the past three years, had gathered so little as not to appreciate this new demand upon them! Had children forgotten father and mother, husbands their wives and little ones!

About this time I was made familiar with a feature of army life to which I have made only slight reference. As a member of a general court-martial, day after day and week after week was occupied in the examination of charges of the gravest character, involving the liberty and life of scores of officers and men. It was the highest tribunal by which those composing the rank and file of the command could be adjudged. Questions of the gravest moment, and of supremest interest to those concerned, were discussed and determined. It was a responsibility shared only by the highest judges in the land, and life and death often hung upon our decisions. A photograph of army life is incomplete without this feature, and while the duty is the gravest and the most solemn which an officer is called upon to perform, it is as necessary to the well-being and efficiency of an army as the ordinary courts of justice to the preservation of the state.

January 30, the Enfans Perdus, an independent battalion, was consolidated into the 47th and 48th New York regiments. The number received by us was about one hundred and fifty. On the 31st, the veterans left for New York, under the charge of several officers. February 4, those left behind received orders to prepare six days' cooked rations, and be in readiness to march, and on the 5th, with the left wing of the 115th New York, they embarked on board the steamer Delaware. On the 6th they left Hilton Head, in company with a number of transports, under the convoy of a gunboat, and proceeded to Florida; the force numbering in all from six to seven thousand men, and comprising artillery, cavalry, and infantry. The artillery and cavalry were under the immediate command of Colonel Henry, and the infantry under Colonels Barton, Hawley, and Scammon, with General Seymour in command of the whole expedition. Its object was to aid the Union people of the state in withdrawing it from Confederate control. General Gilmore accompanied the troops as far as Jacksonville, where they disembarked, and, after seeing that all necessary arrangements were made which could promote the success of the enterprise, returned to Hilton Head, leaving with General Seymour instructions not to attempt an advance beyond Baldwin without further orders, nor unless well assured of success. His intention was to hold and fortify several important points, including Jacksonville, as centres of Federal authority, and reopen those sections to trade. But General Seymour, apparently satisfied that he could not be successfully opposed by any Confederate forces within the state, conceived the idea of destroying the railroad, and cutting off communication with Georgia. As soon as notified of this intended movement, General Gilmore sent a despatch to stop it, but was too late to prevent the massacre which followed. On the 20th a general advance was ordered, and the troops proceeded towards Lake City, about five thousand in all; Colonel Henry with the cavalry in advance, followed by three columns of infantry; Colonel Hawley, with his brigade, on the left; Colonel Barton in the centre; and Colonel Scammon, with his regiment, on the right. In the rear was a brigade of colored troops, under Colonel Montgomery. Near Olustee they came upon a strong force of Confederates favorably posted in the woods, with a swamp in front, over which our troops must pass to reach them. Before they were well aware of the vicinity of the enemy, a murderous fire was opened on them, at a distance of little more than a hundred yards, and for more than two hours they could scarcely do more than stand up to be slaughtered, the nature of the ground and the strength of the enemy effectually preventing any advance. No severer test could be applied to men than they suffered at the battle of Olustee, and when, at evening, the troops were withdrawn, nearly one-fourth of their number were dead or wounded. The most of the latter were left on the field, under the care of Surgeon Defendorf of our regiment, who volunteered to remain with them; an act of bravery and self-sacrifice which cannot be too highly commended. The testimony of those engaged in this affair, as we gather it from journals and other sources, is that it was the most trying position in which they were placed during the war, and the heroism displayed by our men is accounted marvellous. The retreat to Jacksonville was such as might have been expected from broken, dispirited, and defeated troops, with a strong body of the enemy in their rear, flushed with victory, and determined upon their destruction. On the way back, the stores at Baldwin were burned, and when the broken columns were gathered at Jacksonville, it was found that twelve hundred men had been sacrificed, five pieces of artillery and a large number of small arms left in the hands of the Confederates, while the purpose of the government in ordering the expedition was completely frustrated. Our own regiment, whose conduct in the affair was beyond all praise, suffered terribly.

While these events were transpiring, the veterans, and the officers sent with them, were enjoying the comforts of home and the society of friends once more. But the time was all too short, for on the 9th of March we were securely housed in Fort Schuyler, waiting for transportation to the South, which was furnished on the 11th, when we embarked on the steamer Arago, and on the morning of the 16th landed at Hilton Head. Some of us took the opportunity to visit our wounded men in the hospitals. Among them was Sergeant Thompson, whose journal has been of so great service in the composition of this history. It is a pleasure to record of him that he was a faithful soldier, and that, in the recent battle of Olustee, he was conspicuous for coolness and bravery. His services as a soldier ended at this time, and we hope that his subsequent career has been both successful and happy.

Late on the evening of the 16th, we started on the steamer Dictator, to join the other portion of the regiment, which was stationed at Palatka, on the St. John's River, where we arrived on the 18th. The camp was located on the outskirts of the town, and protected by entrenchments. The village consisted of some thirty or forty houses, with three churches, and was almost entirely deserted by its former inhabitants, only a few Union men remaining with their families. Very little occurred, during our stay at Palatka, of special interest. There were occasional alarms, and several attacks by small bodies of Confederates. Pickets were stationed at some distance on the hills back of the town, and the country between was frequently patrolled by guards who were mounted for the purpose.

On the afternoon of the 25th, an expedition was started for the interior, consisting of forty men, with guides, under the command of the writer. We were conveyed up the river about fifteen miles, in the gunboat Ottawa, to what was called Dunn's Creek, through which we proceeded in small boats. The beauty of this stream is impressed on my memory with wonderful distinctness. At its point of junction with the St. John's, and for some little distance, it was narrow, with considerable current, but, as we proceeded, it broadened out, and moved so sluggishly that, at times, it seemed caught and held by the rank growth of grasses and other plants which filled its bed and covered its surface. The branches of the overhanging trees intermingled above our heads, and the pendent moss and dense foliage formed a canopy, through which the sunbeams struggled with dim and softened light, while on either bank the shrubs and trailing vines presented an almost impenetrable wall of bright green leaves and fragrant flowers. Only the songs of birds that fluttered about us broke the stillness, for every one was strangely impressed and subdued by the marvellous beauty by which

A FLORIDA SWAMP AND JUNGLE.

we were surrounded. Silently we pursued our way, except when an occasional opening broke the spell that bound us, until, shooting out of the darkness which had gradually enveloped us, we emerged into the bright moonlight which lighted up the waters of Dunn's Lake. A sharp row of two hours or more brought us to Booth's Landing, where we disembarked. Our object was to capture a few obnoxious individuals who were making special trouble for the Union men who lived in that region; and the night was spent in visits from house to house, much to the discomfort of the inmates. Some very ludicrous scenes occurred, for, while the utmost consideration was used, consistent with the success of our plans, sometimes the occupants of the houses were startled most unceremoniously from their sleep by the tramp of armed men, who entered without knocking, and occupied without permission. A few captures were made, including a Confederate soldier home on leave, and on the following day we rowed back to camp, having accomplished upwards of fifty miles within the twenty-four hours. April 1, one of our pickets was captured, and we never heard of the man afterwards.

April 14, we bade good-by to Palatka, and started for Hilton Head. At Jacksonville we were transferred to the steamer Ben De Ford, and ordered to Beaufort, where we spent a day. On the following day, bidding a final adieu to the Department of the South, we headed for Fortress Monroe, where we made but a brief stop, our destination being Gloucester Point, opposite Yorktown, on the York River.

Glad were we to get into another department, for, from the first, we had felt that, while often performing the most arduous service that falls to the lot of the soldier, the limits of our operations were circumscribed, and the results meagre. Now we were going into the very midst of the conflict. The nature of the change was made manifest by the substitution of shelter tents for those we had been accustomed to use. Each man was served with a single tent, which he carried with his blanket on his back, and by joining with two or three of his comrades, and uniting their tents, a fair shelter or covering could be obtained. The officers were served after the same fashion, the only distinction being that three tents were furnished them instead of one, and they were not compelled to carry their baggage.

Who does not recall the first experience with the shelter tents, into whose openings we were obliged to crawl on our hands and knees to effect an entrance, or the curious sight which the various camps presented, especially at night, when the innumerable sparks of light which dotted the sandy plain seemed to rise

GENERAL GRANT'S HEADQUARTERS AT CITY POINT.

from subterranean caverns, and suggested anything but human habitations? Few were so dull as not to interpret this change from the ample quarters of the Southern Department as meaning for us more active duty, frequent and rapid marches, and fewer comforts. However, there was only a little good-natured grumbling. We all realized that more labor and care would be necessary to preserve arms and equipments in that excellent condition which had elicited such general commendation from the inspectors of the regiment; but it was given cheerfully for the most part, and our reputation for superiority in discipline, drill, and general appearance did not suffer in the comparison with the new troops by whom we were surrounded. General Grant had been made lieutenant-general, and virtually commander-in-chief, and had established his headquarters with the Army of the Potomac. Having shown his ability in many successful campaigns in the West, he was now to contend with a general who easily held the first place in the Confederate service, and with an army long accustomed to victory — fortunately at last, the choice of the President had fallen upon the right man, and he was invested with authority which extended over all the military power of the government. Possessing in a remarkable degree those rare qualities of equanimity and self-possession under all circumstances, he united with these a clear understanding of the condition of the Confederate armies, and the ability to organize and carry forward a well defined and comprehensive plan, which embraced every corps and division in the several departments, by which he was able to hurl against the already weakening forces of the enemy, in simultaneous attacks, the whole power of the Federal army. Allowing little time or opportunity to the enemy for rest or recuperation, he never confessed or accepted defeat.

Our corps, the 10th, was commanded by General Gilmore, while General W. T. Smith commanded the 18th, with which we were associated, the operations of these two being under the direction of General Butler, who commanded the department. April 29, the superfluous baggage of the officers was sent with the company property to Norfolk. April 30, general inspection and review.

At this time General Terry was in command of a division of our corps, and Colonel Barton, who at Hilton Head had been district as well as brigade commander, was in charge of the brigade of which our regiment formed a part, the 47th New York and the 76th and 97th Pennsylvania regiments completing the organization. For General Terry we had already formed a strong attachment. From the time that we met him first, when our regiment was ordered to garrison Fort Pulaski, we had frequently been under him, had watched him through the Morris Island campaign, as temporary commander of the Department of the South, had observed his quiet self-possession, his kindly disposition, and careful forethought for those under him, and had learned to look to him with the respect, confidence, and affection which can only be won by those of superior qualities of mind and heart. We could narrate many incidents in his career, all of which would tend to justify the high estimate in which he is held by the country at large, and, in common with all who have ever served under him, we rejoice in his prosperity, and wish for him a continuance and increase of the favor with which he is justly regarded by the people, whom he has so well served.

CHAPTER XIV.

Bermuda Hundred. Company E as skirmishers. Battle of Chester Heights. Couldn't resist the temptation. Company E fighting on its own account. Bad predicament. Company E did nobly. More fighting. In sight of Richmond. Confederate sharpshooters cleaned out. Battle of Drury's Bluff. Company E again in a bad spot. Wonderful examples of discipline and soldierly conduct. General Terry to the rescue. Retreat. Back to old quarters. Captain Lockwood.

MAY 3 and 4 the regiment did picket duty, and on the 5th left on the steamer Delaware, and sailed down to Fortress Monroe, up the James River, past City Point, to Bermuda Hundred. On the 6th we landed, and, after a brief delay, marched several miles up the Bermuda Hundred road. Early on the morning of the 7th we started again, and, after marching and countermarching for several hours, approached Chester Heights. Behind the hills which concealed us from the enemy, we left our knapsacks, blankets, and other impediments, and the order to advance was received, when we resumed our march, with

Company E thrown out as skirmishers. The instructions received by me from the colonel were general, and somewhat indefinite, the only point well understood being that we were to clear the front of any opposing force. Grasping this idea and at the same time our muskets, we worked our way forward through the woods, until we found ourselves on the top of a hill, with the whole Confederate force in view in the valleys below. But we were entirely separated from our regiment. After vainly endeavoring to take up the connection, we were finally compelled to the conclusion that if we were to have any further part in the affair, it must be by acting independently.

Before us, in the vast amphitheatre, so completely enclosed by the surrounding hills that there seemed no avenue of escape, was the enemy, against whom our attack was directed. Every movement was plainly visible, for not a tree or stone obstructed our view. The utmost activity prevailed, and officers were observed hurrying to and fro, while the changes that followed showed that every preparation would be made to repel attack. One officer, especially, who seemed to be in command, was conspicuous, as he rode about on his white horse, and our men amused themselves for some time in vain attempts to reach him with their rifles, but he was too far away.

As the scene comes back after the lapse of so many years, it seems impossible that the picture imprinted upon the memory can be that of war. That deep, quiet valley, the rich green of its meadows, the protecting hills which circled it, the little hamlets which told their stories of homes, of comfort, and happiness, constituted a picture so peaceful and restful, that those bodies of armed men whose movements we were watching, and the bristling cannon and flashing muskets, seemed strangely out of place.

But there was little time for contemplation. The batteries, one after another, sped up the hill, and, lost for a time, reappeared again, and took position far off to our right, giving us the first intimation of the position of our own troops. Following the same general direction, the several battalions moved up to the support of the batteries, or took positions on the sides of the hills, where they could most effectually resist the advance of our troops. Some two or three of these battalions lay down near the railroad which ran around the valley at the foot of the hills, to be out of the way of our fire, and at the same time be ready to engage in the action if required. These offered altogether too tempting an opportunity to be resisted, and, rushing down to the turnpike, which at this point ran parallel to and very near the railroad, we opened on them a terribly galling and destructive fire. It was a sad predicament, for they could neither return our fire, nor change their position, without exposing themselves to the fire of our main line. When, however, this wavered and fell back, they were at liberty to devote themselves to us, and, with a yell of rage, they precipitated themselves into the deep cut of the railroad, and for a few moments the whistle of bullets about our ears was like the hum of angry bees, whose hive had been disturbed. A large number of Company E of the 7th Connecticut regiment had been doing good work, but with no officer to command them. These joined with our men, and, by carefully availing themselves of such shelter as offered, both companies were brought out of the fiery shower with but slight loss.

Proclamations from headquarters announced the complete success of this expedition, but those who participated in it were unable to discover the success. The whole Confederate force should have been captured, for, once driven into the valley, there could have been no escape for them. Only one division of our corps was engaged, and that not seriously. A portion of the railroad and telegraph line was destroyed, causing a temporary interruption of communication between Richmond and Petersburg. The losses on both sides were small. Dunn, orderly sergeant of Company E, deserves special mention for his coolness and bravery, but every member of Company E is to be commended. Although dreadfully exposed for a few moments, they obeyed orders as if on parade, and it is to their prompt obedience and strict discipline they may impute their safe conduct out of their perilous position. The material of the company was of the best, and it had been specially favored in having such commanders as Coan and

Lockwood. Had Sergeant Dunn showed less soldierly pride (which, however, was very noble in him), he would have avoided the painful wound from which he suffered so long.

On the 8th, we rested; on the 9th, we fought with what were generally called in our camp Gilmore's rifles. In other words, we worked on the intrenchments with picks and spades, and occupied the intrenchments at night. The firing was heavy all about us, and it was rumored that Butler would be able to enter Petersburg in the morning. On the 10th, we shouldered the Gilmore rifles again, but at ten o'clock in the forenoon were ordered to the front, to support Colonel Howell, who was reported falling back; were exposed during the day to the fire of the enemy, but were in much more danger from the fire in the woods, which were burned to clear them from Confederate sharpshooters. Quite an engagement occurred in our front, in which our batteries did fearful execution. General Foster, who went out on flag of truce, reported seeing heaps of Confederate dead in the edge of the woods, many of them half-burned. General Butler did not

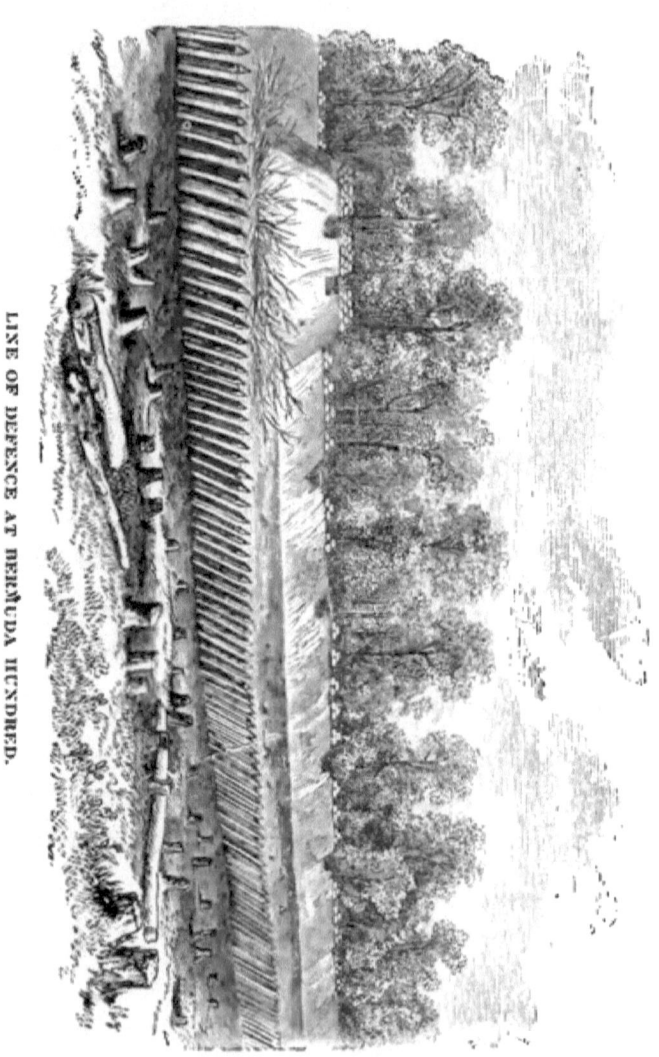

LINE OF DEFENCE AT BERMUDA HUNDRED.

enter Petersburg, being deterred from making any forward movement by the battle in his rear (so it was said).

On the 11th, we rested, and early in the morning of the 12th started away from our intrenchments at Bermuda Hundred, and marched all day in the rain. Rested at night as best we could, with no shelter but the dripping trees (for the rain continued through the night). On the afternoon of the 13th, we moved forward and up to the turnpike, about two miles, where from the tops of the trees those so inclined obtained a view of Richmond and Fort Darling. Again on the 14th, we moved forward into the advance to relieve the 76th Pennsylvania regiment, having up to this time acted as reserve. Our position was about in the centre of the main line, with our right near the Richmond turnpike. Generals Terry and Ames were on the left, and steadily moving forward. That night we occupied the old lines of the Confederates, from which they had been driven by General Gilmore. The 15th was a trying day, for the most of the regiment were out on picket duty, or skirmishing through the woods in our front. The firing of the Confederate sharpshooters, many of whom were stationed in trees, was very annoying, until our men, becoming desperate, hunted them from

PICKETS ON DUTY.

their places of concealment, and before night that mode of warfare was effectually stopped. No quarter was given, and no mercy shown. Still, the firing from the rifle-pits was kept up without intermission, and quite a number of our men were wounded.

Very early on the morning of the 16th, we were conscious that something serious was impending. The irregular firing of musketry was first heard on the extreme right; this was soon followed by regular volleys, mingled with the roar of artillery, and as it continually approached, we knew that it meant a serious disaster to our troops; we could feel the conflict rolling up against us, and quickly disposed our men along the irregular and broken line of wall and fence. Unfortunately, no attempt had been made to construct a regular line of intrenchments, and there was little protection for our troops. About 8 o'clock in the morning, the regiment on our right gave way, and left our flank exposed, and the Confederates poured in upon us in overwhelming numbers, but the brave men of Company E, who held the right of the line, would not give way, but stood their ground as firmly as if no danger threatened, while the Confederates surged in upon them in such masses that it seemed impossible that a single man could escape. The position which they occupied was somewhat in advance of the remainder of the regiment, on a little natural terrace, so that it was some time before the commanding officer was aware of the critical situation in which we were placed, and the order to retire was not received until that little knoll was literally covered with the dead and dying. Corporals Smalls and Brassell, and poor Jockers, the brave little man from the Enfans Perdus, with eleven others, lay dead or wounded, while others, less severely injured, had made their way to the rear.

In the very hottest of the fire, Lawson, the orderly sergeant of the company, hobbled up to where I was stationed, and, saluting, said, "I am wounded, sir." "Go to the rear" was the reply. A ball had passed completely through his thigh. Corporal Barton, almost for the first time in battle, having, for the most part, been employed as a clerk at division or corps headquarters, came to me, and, saluting, exhibited his wound, while every line of his countenance told the anguish he was suffering. A ball had shattered his hand while he was in the act of loading; but he would not go to the rear without the order of his commanding officer. Never shall I forget the brave soldier Vreeland,

FORT DARLING.

who, stationed behind the little apple-tree, continued loading and firing, until fairly dragged away, so grievously wounded that there was no hope of recovery. As I write, I feel that every name in that heroic band, the living and the dead, should be inscribed in letters of gold on the pages of history. Such faithfulness, such heroism, such discipline, I never saw exhibited elsewhere. Better soldiers never lived; braver men never died. Not a man left that knoll without permission till the order came to retreat. But what confusion followed! Who of those present will not recall that struggling mass of broken regiments; hopeless, and distracted, until the cool self-possession of General Terry brought order out of the confusion, and led the way out to safety and security. Not a moment too soon, for as we toiled our weary way up the hillside, the shot and shell from the Confederate batteries in the turnpike made many avenues through the retreating columns. And very glad were we when the distance and intervening hills secured us from further annoyance.

We should here state that the right of the

line, which was the first to give way before the Confederate assault, was under the command of General Wright; while the left of the line, under General Terry, resisted every attack, and only retreated when the danger of being cut off and captured became imminent. That night we spent in our old camp, near the intrenchments at Bermuda Hundred; and the following day rested. On the 18th, did some picket and skirmish duty, and on the 19th were still in the front, enjoying the music of shot and shell; and to the 28th, there was little rest, night or day, between fatigue, picket, and skirmish duty. The enemy made frequent attacks on our outer lines, but without success; and we could observe them for the most of the time engaged in constructing intrenchments. General Butler was not accomplishing the work allotted to him. Petersburg was not taken, and no important advantage had been gained.

On the 25th, Captain Lockwood left us, to return to civil life. It was a great loss to the regiment, for he was a good officer, an intelligent man, an agreeable companion, and a loyal friend. The places of the old officers, so many of whom have fallen in battle or have voluntarily left the service, cannot be filled. They were royal men, who were borne into the service by that first fresh, pure wave of patriotism which swept over the North in the earliest days of the war. Of them all, Lockwood was my most intimate friend — respected, trusted, and beloved. Returning home, he engaged in the business of manufacturing, in which he continued until his death, which occurred some years after the war closed. He and Lieutenant-Colonel Strickland were law partners in New York city at the breaking-out of the war.

CHAPTER XV.

Assigned to 6th corps. On the way to the Army of the Potomac. A dreadful march. At Cold Harbor. Trying situation. Assume command. A gallant charge. Grand success. Severe losses. Driven back. Lack of support. Incidents of the battle. The demoralized general. Further account of Cold Harbor. Occupying the Confederate line. A sad picture of war. An uncomfortable situation. Relieved. Close work. Change of base. Grand but perilous movement of the army. The old church at Jamestown.

On the evening of the 28th, we broke camp, and marched all night towards City Point, which we reached about daylight on the morning of the 29th. We remained there until afternoon, when, having embarked on the steamer Delaware, we proceeded down the river. By this time, it had become generally understood that our division of the 10th corps had been temporarily united with the 18th corps, and that we were on our way to join the Army of the Potomac. About the middle of the forenoon of the 31st, we landed at the White House, on the Pamunkey River. Here rations were distributed, the men got their dinners, and late in the afternoon the order was given to fall in.

Nearly all night was spent on the march; and when we halted it was not to rest, but to do picket duty. Early on the morning of June 1, we resumed our march, and continued all day, resting occasionally, as the men became too exhausted to keep on. The heat was almost intolerable, and the dust so filled the air that at

GENERAL SMITH'S HEADQUARTERS, COLD HARBOR.

times it was impossible to see the distance of a company front ahead of us. When the command to halt was given, the regiment seemed to melt away, and it was with the utmost difficulty that the march could be resumed. Many men were reported as fatally exhausted and left to die by the roadside from the commands that had preceded us, and it required the combined efforts of our own officers, and the example of patient and cheerful endurance on their part, to keep our men from falling away and straggling. Arrived at Cold Harbor, late in the afternoon, we were ordered into the woods — as we supposed, to encamp. But alas! a soldier may never rest, till he or the enemy is dead.

After standing in line, with arms stacked, for a half-hour, the order came to move forward to engage in an attack on the enemy's works, first from the brigade commander, afterwards from the division, and finally from corps headquarters. The 47th New York regiment, which was on our left, had already moved away, and still no word of command was given. What should we do? The greatest excitement prevailed. Finally, in the absence of Major Coan, who had been detailed on special duty, and at the earnest solicitations of several officers, the writer assumed command, although not the ranking officer present. The situation was peculiar, and the emergency desperate; and when the order was given to take arms, they were seized with an alacrity which told of the feeling that prevailed. The officers expressed their satisfaction, and the men moved with a promptness which signified the relief they felt for their rescue from the impending disgrace. "Shoulder arms! Left face! Forward march! By the right flank, march! Left oblique! Double quick!" and we had joined the brigade. "Charge bayonets!" across the field, and into the woods; and the first line of the enemy's rifle-pits was occupied. Here the men stopped, and commenced firing; but a lull in the fire of the enemy enforced the order to move forward, and in little more time than it takes to write it we had captured and occupied a section of the main line of Confederate works, and had more prisoners marching to the rear than the whole number present in the regiment. Will any of our readers recall the name of the little corporal of Company G, scarce five feet high, at whose command, as he stood on the top of the works, at charge bayonet, "Come out of there, you d—d rebels," a lieutenant and nearly a dozen men emerged from the works, and humbly and quietly proceeded to the rear with the other prisoners?

How much was crowded into the short time that we occupied that line of intrenchments. Lieutenant Ingraham, for the first time in action, having heretofore been detailed in the commissary department, with many others, was shot in the very moment of victory. It was a dreadful place to hold, with the rebels massed just at the foot of the hill, on the right, and pouring in upon us a deadly flanking fire. Repeated messages were sent to the commanding general, explaining our situation, and urging an attack on our right, or re-enforcements to enable us to do it; but no help, and no word of any kind, was received. Efforts were made to induce the commander of the 47th New York, which was separated from us by a little ravine on our left, to unite with us in a charge down the hill; but without avail, for either our purpose was misunderstood owing to the distance between us, which made communication difficult, or disinclination or positive orders forbade, and so we were compelled to wait and suffer, hoping that some general officer would become interested to find our whereabouts, and organize some new move-

POSITION OF GENERAL SMITH'S COMMAND AT COLD HARBOR, VA.

ment, by which we would be relieved. The order to charge down the hill would have been welcome, but it would have been madness to have attempted it without support. While we waited, and our numbers were rapidly diminishing, we could plainly see the Confederate reserves gathering in the distance, across the meadow at the foot of the hill, and knew that we could not hold our position long unless help came.

At this time, the adjutant-general of the brigade that had charged across the same ground that we had come over, came to me, and offered his services, stating that his brigade had been routed and scattered, and nearly all the field officers of the command killed or wounded. While explaining to him the position of affairs, and urging him to go to the rear and endeavor to hurry up re-enforcements, a bullet pierced his brain, and he sank in death. I remember Corporal St. John of Company G, who, finding a sword which had belonged to a rebel officer, kindly presented it to me, as unmindful of the bullets which whistled about our heads as if they were not freighted with missions of death to himself or comrades. Of such men was the regiment composed. But, as the shadows deepened about us, there came a rush. The enemy was fairly upon us; and, before we could gather ourselves to repel the attack, some one, without authority, had called out to retreat, and, in the confusion which followed, the colors were seized and held by the enemy, not, however, without a fierce but hopeless struggle. Back through the woods we went, broken and dispirited. After securing a victory, we had been left alone and unsupported, to be shot down like sheep, and the men knew that it was time to seek a place of shelter.

There was a rally at the edge of the woods, where we found the commander of a division reclining under a tree, apparently deserted by every one, and in a state of complete helplessness and demoralization. Although he has since occupied positions of great prominence and responsibility, we never hear his name without recalling his appearance, when, emerging from the woods, we discovered him in the situation described, and learned his name and rank. Completely beside himself because of the defeat and dispersion of his command, he insisted that the feeble line of officers and men who collected in his vicinity should renew the attack, when a whole division had been defeated and scattered. Fairly out of the sound of his voice, we left him to his own reflections. Already darkness had settled down upon us, and, after a little council of war, with Lieutenant Barrett and others, we lay down for a little rest, in the field over which the regiment had so gallantly charged that afternoon. It had done nobly, and, with the other regiments of the brigade, can claim the only substantial success attained by the division; for we believe they were the only troops who succeeded in capturing the main line of rebel intrenchments.

At the point which we occupied, this line passed across the top of a hill, which sloped down to a meadow in front, and on the right dropped more abruptly, to what seemed quite a deep ravine. The Federal line stopped with the right of our regiment, and evidently no successful attack, if any at all, had been made on our immediate right. After we commenced our charge across the field, no communication whatever was received from our commanding officers, while it has always seemed to the writer that, if the success which we attained had been followed up, most important results would have been achieved. It is possible that the troops who preceded us in the attack reached the first line of the enemy's rifle-pits, for at that point we met with little opposition. But they penetrated no farther, and, either unaware of their partial success, or exhausted in the effort, they became so completely scattered that we saw no trace of them.

The next day, June 2, the remnant of the regiment capable of duty was ordered to occupy a portion of the Confederate line, to the left of that captured by us the night before. As we filed through the woods, we passed a little pale-faced boy. Separated from his comrades, he struggled on through the underbrush. with wearied steps, uncared-for and alone. His feeble hands scarce held the musket which he dragged along. All his remaining consciousness seemed concentrated on the effort to do as others did, and as we hurried past him, he turned on us a dazed, bewildered look. We could not stop, else we would have taken him by the hand, and led him away from the danger he was in, to the protection and care of comrades and friends, as we longed to do. We found him when we came back, but he had passed beyond the sphere of human sympathy and aid. The look of painful weariness was gone from that little upturned face. He had found rest. It seems strange, but that picture is burned into the memory with such distinctness that it comes up before the eye whenever the touch of recollection brings back the incidents of army life. That day, on those intrenchments, we lay down beside the dead and dying of the regiment relieved, to serve as targets for the enemy, who were close at hand, and familiar with the locality. We did not remain long, and were glad to get away. During our stay, the greatest precaution was necessary, on account of the near vicinity of the enemy. Lieutenant Barrett, who was always at the point of danger, while obeying the order of the commanding officer to lie down behind the log which lay across the path, at the foot of the intrenchments, received a painful wound, which kept him in hospital for months afterwards. A member of company G, who had sheltered himself behind a stump, which rose about two feet above the top of the earthworks, received, as he supposed, his death-wound, and gave audible expression to his dying agonies, but, as the effect of the shot, which had nearly spent itself in the rotten stump, passed off, the sharp whizzing of a bullet, which came uncomfortably near his head, brought him to life so suddenly that, starting up with a spring, he darted away for the intrenchments as if the Evil One were following, and did not fully recover his senses until he found himself in a place of safety, outside the wood. The nature of the situation in which we were placed may be judged by the order which I was constrained to give in respect to the manner of retiring when we were relieved; namely, that the men should go out one at a time from the extreme left of the line, hugging closely to the earthwork as they crawled to this point. This was accomplished without a single casualty, and the writer resumed command just outside the danger line, where he found the regiment formed as if for parade. It was a constant pleasure to be associated with such officers in the command of such men. That night we remained under arms near our intrenchments, which had been thrown up after our repulse of the day previous. From the journals before me, I learn that the casualties in the regiment, during the twenty-four hours, were five officers killed, four wounded, and eighty enlisted men killed, wounded and missing,— a very large proportion of those engaged, especially of officers.

June 3, no special duty, but frequently moved from one point to another along our works. Some hard fighting was going on near us at different times in the day, and we were constantly under an irregular but annoying fire. June 4, moved up into an exposed position in the rear of our advanced line of works. June 5, although the men built intricate lines of rifle-pits, with most ingenious contrivances for protection, they were still very much exposed, and several were wounded. In the evening occupied the very front line. A sharp attack was made on our left, but without avail. During the afternoon of the 6th, the firing ceased for a little while, and we had an opportunity of seeing the Confederate works, which in our immediate front were somewhat disconnected and not as strong as ours. It had been dangerous to expose even a hand, so close were the Confederates, and so sharp the firing; and it was good to be relieved from this for a few moments. When the short truce was over, some of our men commenced singing, "We'll hang Jeff Davis on a sour apple-tree," which so enraged the Johnnies that they made it warm for us until the singing ceased.

The 7th was a quiet day, but we had need of watchfulness. The 9th corps, under Burnside, was on our right, and formed the right flank of the Federal army. In front of some parts of our lines, the Confederate works were apparently within a hundred yards, and extreme precautions were necessary to guard against a sudden rush. Men were stationed outside, in rifle-pits, so near that they talked with the Confederates similarly posted. These men could only be relieved in the darkness of the night. This evening the bands played all along our lines, not funeral dirges, but airs of joy and triumph, telling us that something important had occurred, or was about to occur.

The 8th and 9th were, comparatively speaking, days of rest. The woods between us and the 9th corps had been cut down, to make the connection more perfect. Our position and duties continued about the same until the night of the 11th, when extra precautions indicated that something was going on. On the 12th, the air was full of rumors, and it was soon understood that the whole army was about to change its base of operations. Just at dark, the 76th Pennsylvania, on our left, moved out of the rifle-pits, and their places were occupied by our regiment. At the same time, we were informed that the 9th corps had already left, and we should be the last to go. The constant yells and the heavy firing of the Confederates indicated that they suspected something unusual, and we prepared ourselves for an attack on our weakened line. The utmost vigilance was exercised, for every one knew the extreme peril of our situation, and when, at one o'clock on the morning of the 13th, the order came to evacuate, every voice was hushed. The whispered word was passed from man to man, to retire from the works one by one from the left, in perfect silence, and rendezvous in the woods some distance in the rear; seven companies thus moved out, without accident, or casualty, although the shot and shell shrieked about our heads continually. But the most delicate task remained — namely, the extricating the three companies who, as outpost sentinels and sharpshooters, were so near the enemy that it seemed impossible for them to escape. This, however, was accomplished, with the loss of a few men, who were necessarily left behind, and we took up our line of march for the White House, occupying the most honorable position in this perilous movement, when the whole Federal army was withdrawn from the immediate presence of Lee's army, without its knowledge and without serious loss. It has been well remarked, by an able writer on military operations, that it was one of the most remarkable movements in the annals of warfare, and could not have been carried out successfully except by the most experienced troops, under the most perfect training and discipline.

Early on the morning of the 14th, we steamed away from the White House on the Pamunkey River in two small transports on our return to Bermuda Hundred. During our

BATTERY AND CHURCH TOWER. SITE OF JAMESTOWN.

voyage, we passed within sight of the ruins of the old church at Jamestown. How full of suggestion and reflection, recalling, as they did, the history of the proud old state, with its long line of distinguished patriots, soldiers, and statesmen. We thought of Patrick Henry, whose glowing eloquence first set ablaze the smouldering embers of rebellion, and of Washington, whose wisdom, endurance, and constancy, sealed at Yorktown the title to independence, and the inalienable rights of manhood to life, liberty, and the pursuit of happiness, and wondered at the inconsistency and blindness of the early fathers of our country, who permitted the ingrafting of the gigantic, festering evil of slavery upon our system of government, thereby entailing on us the sufferings and horrors, the changes and uncertainties, of this war. All the more singular because liberty and justice were the foundation principles of church, state, and society. During the voyage to Bermuda Hundred, the transports became separated, and the morning of the 16th found only one wing of the regiment arrived at its destination. This was immediately ordered outside the intrenchments, to the Confederate picket-line, which had been evacuated during the night.

CHAPTER XVI.

Back to Bermuda Hundred. A running fight. Destruction of railroad. Kindness of Major Young and General Terry. Ordered to charge. A happy escape. President Lincoln and General Butler. Ordered to attack Confederate line. Recalled. Captain Fee and others killed. Picket-lines at Petersburg. Sanitary and Christian Commissions. Mine explosion. Our losses. Major Swartwout. Effects of malaria.

OF our change of base, conducted so cautiously and secretly, the enemy did not continue long in ignorance. All day we were running against the troops, ordered from the South to anticipate us in the occupancy of Petersburg. Firing was going on continually, and the only effective service that we rendered was the destruction of the railroad. Even this was only partial, as we had neither time nor appliances, for thorough work. The section of the road upon which our battalion operated was on the side of a hill, and the men being placed near together along the track, at the word of command, seized, lifted, and tumbled down the hill, the portion spanned by the line, ties and rails going together, leaving the road-bed clean. This was repeated, until the appearance of the enemy in large numbers warned us that we should move, and move quickly, which we did. At night the men were completely exhausted, and without food, all the stores belonging to the regiment being on the steamer with the field and staff. It was plainly my duty to see that they were supplied with rations — but there was no one to whom I could apply, except General Terry, and his headquarters were miles away. I had no conveyance, and there was no one near whom I knew. The nearest regiment was the 142d Ohio, under command of Major Young. There was no alternative, and I was compelled to apply to him for means of transportation. Although a stranger, there was little need of explanation before his horse stood ready at his tent. General Terry responded most cheerfully to my request, and by midnight the men were enjoying the simple food which served them for the next day of labor or suffering. Neither of these officers knew what a kindly act they did that night; but had they witnessed the distribution of stores to those famishing men, who waited patiently till midnight for my return, they would have been fully repaid for their kindness. The result of the day's operations was the destruction of quite a large section of the railroad, and the capture of some fifty or more prisoners.

On the 17th, the remainder of the brigade landed at Bermuda Hundred, and the regiment encamped near the intrenchments. Towards evening were ordered out to charge the enemy's intrenchments, and for an hour lay on the side of a hill, watching the movements of the brigade whose place we were to take in case it was not successful. What we witnessed was not at all inspiriting; for, as the smoke lifted from the first heavy discharge of the Confederate artillery and musketry, we looked in vain for any sign of our troops, who seemed to have been completely annihilated. To take their place was not to be looked upon as a privilege; and when the order was received to return to camp, we were not reluctant to go. It should be said, by way of explanation, that our loss was very slight, the order to lie down having been given in season to avoid the shot and shell, which passed harmlessly over our troops. Why they did not rise and charge immediately was never explained to us.

On the 18th, we remained encamped near the intrenchments. The 18th and 6th corps were

BATTERY NEAR DUTCH GAP.

in our vicinity, while the 2d, 5th, and 9th were near Petersburg. We heard heavy firing, but could learn nothing definite concerning the progress of our army.

On the afternoon of the 22d, a message was received from General Butler that President Lincoln was approaching our vicinity, and would shortly reach the point where we were encamped. The purpose of the message was to give time and opportunity to arrange a fitting welcome, but it was unfortunate that nearly all the troops in our neighborhood were hundred-days men, who, having been enlisted to do duty within their respective states, had been forced into the Army of the Potomac, and pushed into the most perilous service, in violation of their contract. For this reason they were much disaffected, and one regiment, at least, had been deprived of its arms, and placed under guard, to prevent a serious outbreak. Naturally, the message of General Butler was received by them very coldly, and as the cavalcade surrounding the President appeared, there were but few straggling squads of soldiers in sight, and from these there was no sign of enthusiasm or interest. I have seen General Butler many times, and under a variety of conditions and surroundings, but never so completely disconcerted as then. As the party neared the point where we stood, an aid was hurriedly sent forward to command the men to cheer, and General Butler, dropping behind the President, endeavored, by frantic gestures and pantomime, to enforce the orders of his aid. But all to no purpose. The men were angry and sullen, and when the general, rising in his stirrups, shook his fist at them, the exhibition of impotent rage was greeted with shouts of derision. As the little cavalcade advanced farther along the line, an effort was made by the other troops in the vicinity to make amends to our honored and beloved President for this discourtesy; but, while the whole army was intensely loyal, and devotedly attached to him, he was unfortunate in having, as his chief escort through our lines, a general who had, at least temporarily, lost the confidence and respect of the command.

On the 23d, the regiment was ordered to join that portion of the army in front of Petersburg. Nothing unusual occurred until the 30th, when we were ordered to prepare for a charge on the Confederate works. Instead of remaining where we were, protected by our intrenchments, until the charge was ordered, we were moved over our earthworks, where we were kept for some time, exposed to a murderous

the President, endeavored, by frantic gestures and pantomime, to enforce the orders of his aid. But all to no purpose. The men were angry and sullen, and when the general, rising in his stirrups, shook his fist at them, the exhibition of impotent rage was greeted with shouts of derision. As the little cavalcade advanced farther along the line, an effort was made by the other troops in the vicinity to make amends to our honored and beloved President for this discourtesy; but, while the whole army was intensely loyal, and devotedly attached to him, he was unfortunate in having, as his chief escort through our lines, a general who had, at least temporarily, lost the confidence and respect of the command.

On the 23d, the regiment was ordered to join that portion of the army in front of Petersburg. Nothing unusual occurred until the 30th, when we were ordered to prepare for a charge on the Confederate works. Instead of remaining where we were, protected by our intrenchments, until the charge was ordered, we were moved over our earthworks, where we were kept for some time, exposed to a murderous

fire, by which Captain Fee, a brave and excellent officer, and many others, were killed or severely wounded. After nearly a half-hour of this exposure, we were recalled, and the attack was given up, as well it might be after our intention was so fairly made known to the enemy.

At this time the main lines of the two armies were in such close proximity that the utmost care was necessary, especially on the part of the pickets who were posted in the little valley between, and were so near that no part of the body could be exposed for an instant without drawing the fire of the enemy. The approach to the picket-line was through intricate and carefully protected, covered ways, but, with all the precautions which ingenuity could devise, day by day our ranks were diminished by losses. Many of these occurred in the passage to and from these picket-lines, and often were due to the recklessness and carelessness of the men. Many and curious were the devices used to draw the enemy's fire, by exposing a hat, or coat, or other object, while, from ingeniously constructed lookouts, our men watched for the heads which were sure to pop up from behind their intrenchments in the eagerness for a shot. This brutal warfare was kept up during our whole stay in front of Petersburg, except when a short truce brought the picket-lines together, when the utmost freedom of intercourse prevailed. At such times papers were exchanged, the situation discussed, and the best of friends seemed engaged in mutual congratulations. In a few moments, the old state of things was resumed, with all its cruelties.

At this time more than ever before, we realized the magnitude of the works performed by the Sanitary and Christian Commissions. As an illustration, I find it recorded in my journal that at this time our whole army was supplied with vegetables by the Sanitary Commission; while the agents of both societies were to be found in camp and hospital, ministering to the sick, wounded, and needy, with a generous impartiality, which made no distinctions, and shrunk neither from danger by bullet or contaminating disease. It is not my province to enter into a history of these societies; but I should be ungrateful did I not make fitting acknowledgment of the good work performed by those devoted Christian men and women. Not only were the officers and soldiers largely benefited as individuals, but the army, as a whole, was sustained and strengthened by the knowledge that through these two societies, and others of similar character, the whole people were manifesting

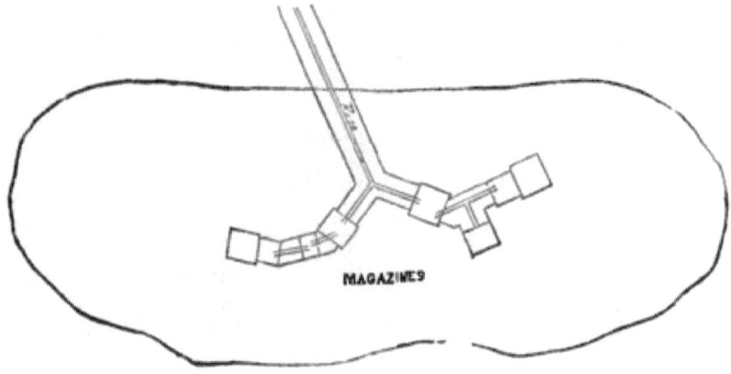

OUTLINE OF THE CRATER AND MAGAZINES.

their readiness to bear their share of burden and sacrifice. The office which they performed, in establishing and sustaining a higher moral standard in the army, and the increased efficiency which resulted from it, cannot be overestimated.

During the most of July, we occupied the front or rear lines before Petersburg, under fire the most of the time, the shot and shell reaching us even in the most protected spots. The men were picked off by sharpshooters whenever within range, and there was no respite from duty, although we participated in no regular engagement until the 30th. At sunset on the 29th, the regiment took up its line of march to the left and rear, to be ready to join in the attack which was to be made immediately after the explosion of the mine in front of the 9th corps. The explosion took place between four and five o'clock on the morning of the 30th, and the attack was made; but, owing to want of preparation, or some lack in the arrangement, the favorable moment was allowed to pass, and the charge was irregular and ineffective. After advancing to the ground which had been occupied by the fort, a halt was made, intrenchments thrown up, and two guns mounted. This gave an opportunity for the enemy to rally, and when at last the charge was made upon Cemetery Hill, which was immediately in front, and some four hundred yards distant, the concentrated fire from the front, and from either flank, ploughed through our lines, creating disorder and confusion. The loss was dreadful, regiments and brigades being almost completely annihilated; a second attempt only added to a disaster which was one of the most serious that our army had suffered for months. Our division had been joined to the 18th corps, which made a demonstration on the right, but without avail. Our losses were severe. Among the killed was Major Swartwout, one of the oldest and best of all the officers who had been connected with the regiment. No one among us possessed to a larger extent the real soldierly instincts, and no one was more generally beloved. His genial good-nature, his ready humor, and exuberant spirits, made him welcome in every circle. Lieutenant O'Brien was also killed, and our loss otherwise, in non-commissioned officers and privates, was severe. The scheme, which originated with Lieutenant-Colonel Pleasants, of the 48th Pennsylvania regiment, was well conceived and perfected by him; but the attack which followed the explosion was managed badly.

July 31, the regiment was ordered to Bermuda Hundred, where we remained until

August 13, when we broke camp, and, starting late in the evening, marched all night. The writer's experience on that night march was peculiar, and, as showing the severity of the duties to which we had been subjected, and the condition to which many of us were reduced, it may properly be mentioned. The command of the regiment devolved upon me, owing to the absence of all the field officers. Starting at its head, we had proceeded but a short distance before I was seized by an attack of drowsiness, which no effort and no expedient could throw off. Mortified beyond expression by this singular but uncontrollable weakness, there was nothing left to me, at last, but an appeal to the orderly, and, directing him to keep me in my proper position, and to arouse me if anything special should occur, I gave up the useless struggle. The false or heavy step of the horse which I was riding aroused me frequently to sudden consciousness, when the struggle would recommence, but with the same result, for the seeds of malaria, brought from the swamps of the Savannah, were fruiting in a deadly exhaustion, which no effort of the will could overcome. This was the precursor of more serious attacks, which finally drove me from the service. Our movement was in the direction of the Dutch Gap Canal, a project of General Butler, which proved a failure, like many others of his undertakings while in the service.

CHAPTER XVII.

On duty at the front. Strange sickness. General Grant under fire. Captain D'Arcy. Battle of Strawberry Plains. Splendid behavior of the regiment. Lieutenants Tantum and Sears picked off by Confederate sharpshooters. Other losses. The excited officer. Hurried retreat. Captain Taylor. The greeting of General Terry. A night's rest. On picket duty. Sad condition of the regiment. Expiration of term of enlistment. Disaffection. Severe duty. Artillery attack on Petersburg. Out of the service.

WE have never heard of any general order issued to the army annulling the Fourth Commandment, but such had been our experience that we needed no argument to persuade us, on the morning of the 14th of August, which was the Sabbath, that some special service, in field or camp, would be required. All day long, we were at the front, in plain sight and within range of a Confederate battery. The weather was intensely hot, and a most curious effect followed the long exposure to the glaring sun. Many officers, as well as non-commissioned officers and privates, succumbed to the heat, and were led or carried to the rear. Some were taken with spasms, and sometimes whole groups fell together; but, the surgeon being summoned, a wonderful change took place, and the powerful remedies which he administered to the most marked cases seemed to have a peculiar effect on the others. It was a remarkable experience, and I have never been able fully to explain the nature of the attack. For a time it seemed likely that we should have a battalion of invalids; but the illness was of short duration, and no serious results followed. While occupying a little hill, the top of which was crossed by a stone wall, General Grant made his appearance, with General Barnard and other members of his staff. Passing through our ranks, he ascended the hill to the stone wall, where he remained some time, taking observations. In the meantime, the battery across the meadow kept up a constant fire, and General Grant was often obliged to duck his head behind the wall to avoid the shot. One of these, which had passed uncomfortably near him, proved fatal to Captain D'Arcy, who was just returning from the valley below, with some of those who had retired under the effect of the sunstroke. He was a good officer, but sometimes showed the want of coolness and self-possession. This would undoubtedly have come to him with age and longer experience. With this, he would have been an officer of unusual excellence; for he was well informed, of quick perceptions, and prompt in all his movements, while his bravery was beyond question. The only result of the day's work, of which we had any report, was the capture of a battery and fifty prisoners by General Terry. The next day, the 15th, we were moved from point to point continually, but were not engaged.

On the next day, the 16th, occurred the battle of Strawberry Plains, where our loss was very severe. I copy from my journal: "During the forenoon moved to the left in rear of battery. Remained a little while, and then moved to the right through the woods. On the way, the firing became heavy in our front, and we soon got the order to double-quick. Through the woods, over dead bodies, — Federals and Confederates mingled together, — past lines of prisoners, into the open ground, knapsacks thrown off, full of enthusiasm, away we went, forming behind the Confederate works, by the right into line, as straight and true as ever on parade drill, amid the cheering of the troops about us. Men, cheerful, cool, and obedient, under a heavy fire, in which Lieutenant John M. Tantum, of Company D, a Christian man and good soldier, was killed, and Seward, Sears, and many others, wounded. We stuck to the works until the regiments on our right and left had fled, and only gave way when the Confederates were so near that we could almost feel their breath."

During the day we witnessed a marked illustration of the necessity for coolness, as well as bravery, especially on the part of officers. Our position was a trying one, for, although there was no enemy in sight, we were under a heavy enfilading fire, probably from sharpshooters stationed in the trees of the adjoining woods, and we had reason to expect an attack, either in front or flank, at any moment. Under the circumstances, it was necessary that the command should be well in hand, cool, alert, and ready for any emergency. While we were closely hugging the intrenchments, to avoid as far as possible the enemy's fire, every man grasping his musket, and waiting for the word of command, a staff officer, possessing more courage than discretion, came along, with pistol in one hand and sword in the other, and gave the order to commence firing. In an instant the men were on their feet, and the utmost confusion prevailed. The firing which followed indicated more perfectly the position of our regiment to the enemy, who were themselves so completely concealed in the woods at our left that no return fire could be effectual. Worse than all, our men could only fire directly to the front,— where as yet there was no sign of the enemy,— on account of the regiment which at that time connected with our left flank. As long as the firing continued, the advantage of preparations to repel attack was entirely lost, and it was only by threats of immediate personal injury that the officer was induced to take his ill-timed enthusiasm elsewhere, and order was restored. In our retreat, which occurred soon after, Captain Taylor was the only officer left to assist in the command of the regiment; and, as we hurried through the woods, a last look behind discovered several Confederate battle-flags close at hand, and already occupying the position we had just left. How heartily we congratulated each other on our escape, when so many of our friends and comrades had fallen; but only an hour afterwards, our picket-lines having been established, and placed in his charge, word was brought to me that he too had been grievously wounded. It was a sad blow, and left me in a very embarrassing position; for the enemy was pressing hard upon us. Soon, however, several officers, who, for various reasons, had been absent during the day, reported for duty; but no one who took his place. Always ready for whatever he was called upon to do, he was cheerful and intelligent in its performance. An excellent officer, and most agreeable companion. This was his third wound, and, although he recovered sufficiently to attend to ordinary business, he was obliged to leave the service. His constitution was much shattered, and gradually gave way, under the combined effects of his wounds and the malarial disorders contracted in the army. Never shall I forget the greeting of General

Terry as we emerged from the woods. He had seen our good regiment through the whole affair, and his plaudit of "well done" was honest and hearty. There was no rest that night, but when, at the close of the following day, the 17th, after much wearisome marching, we sank down on the damp ground, wet, hungry, and exhausted, many a prayer of thanksgiving went up to Him who had spared us, where so many had fallen by our sides. On the 18th, there was fighting in our front, but we were not engaged.

Having got back to the intrenchments at Deep Bottom, we were allowed a short season of rest. Heavy firing was continually going on about us, especially in the direction of Petersburg; but, although so near, we received no reliable accounts of what was transpiring.

On the 20th we left Deep Bottom, and for a portion of the day acted as a picket guard. The line was formed across Strawberry Plains and the duty was a delicate one, as our troops were retreating over the roads by which the enemy was expected. The following day we marched to our old camp-ground at Bermuda Hundred.

During the week just passed, we had lost Captain D'Arcy, Lieutenants Tantum and Sears, killed, and Captain Taylor and Lieutenant Seward, wounded, while Lieutenant Acker was in hospital, suffering from sunstroke. Many non-commissioned officers and privates had been killed and wounded, while others, officers and soldiers, were incapacitated for duty.

About this time there arose much disaffection in the regiment among those men who, having served three years, demanded their discharge. While sympathizing fully with their feelings, although the commanding officer, it was impossible for me to relieve them from duty, especially as at this time we were taxed to our utmost in guarding a long line, which had previously been occupied by a whole brigade. A few cases of discipline were necessary, but, for the most part, the men were amenable to reason, and recognized the necessity of performing service until relieved by competent authority. On the 24th, we moved farther to the right, and every man was put on picket. At this time there were but three officers present for duty. Chills and fever were very prevalent, and the regiment was reduced to a skeleton of its former self. Early on the morning of the 25th, a sharp attack was made on our picket-line, but was repulsed. Our loss was one man killed, and nine wounded and missing. Rumors prevailed for several days that we were to be sent to Petersburg, and on Sunday, the 28th, the order came, and by nine o'clock of that evening we were in our old quarters. On the evening of the 29th, the batteries on the hills back of us opened a heavy fire on Petersburg, and continued for some time. It was a magnificent sight. The air was alive with shells, and in their flight they seemed to rise even to the stars, and to mingle their light with them. From this time until September 14, the duties of the regiment were without variety or special interest. With the 76th Pennsylvania, it alternated in serving at the front and resting in the rear lines. On the 14th, my connection with the regiment ceased. After more than three years of service, completely broken down by malarial disease contracted in the early period of the war, at my urgent request I was permitted to resign. What follows of this history has been largely drawn from the journals of others, and several histories of the war, which I have constantly consulted in preparing this narrative.

CHAPTER XVIII.

Discharge of old members of the regiment. Attack at Chapin's Farm. Partial success. Condition of the South. New recruits. In winter-quarters. Thanksgiving Day. Resignation of Colonel Barton. His long and faithful service. Tenth and Eighteenth corps united. Expedition against Fort Fisher. Second expedition against Fort Fisher. Gallant charge and capture of the fort. An important event. Other successes. March to Wilmington. Pursuit of the Confederates. Their surrender of Union prisoners. Their condition. On the march to join Sherman's army. Sherman's grand march to the sea-coast, and its results. Grant's operations ending in surrender of Lee and his army. With Sherman's army on the march for Johnston. Announcement of surrender of General Lee. Continued pursuit of Johnston. Lincoln's assassination. Its effect on the army. Surrender of Johnston.

SEPTEMBER 17, the old members of the regiment who had not re-enlisted were honorably discharged, and started homewards. On the 28th, the 10th and 18th corps left the intrenchments at Petersburg, and, crossing the Appomattox, marched to the James River. The 10th corps, under General Birney, was to attack the enemy at Deep Bottom, while to the 18th corps, under General Ord, was assigned the duty of taking the Confederate works at Chapin's Farm. The 10th corps made an assault early on the morning of the 29th, and were completely successful; but the 18th corps, after gallantly carrying the outer works at Chapin's Farm, and capturing fifteen pieces of artillery and many prisoners, found the second line of defence so formidable that more careful

ARMY'S HUTS AT CHAPIN'S FARM.

preparations were necessary before attempting its capture. In the meantime, General Birney proceeded up the Newmarket road towards Richmond, and established communication with the 18th corps. The delay which followed the first assault at Chapin's Farm, gave time for the enemy to call in re-enforcements, and the second assault proved unsuccessful. The following day the enemy attempted to recover the portion of the works which they had lost, but were repulsed with considerable loss. In these engagements, the 48th lost a number of men, in killed, wounded, and prisoners.

October 7, a vigorous effort was made by the enemy to drive us out of our positions on the north side of the James, but, after a partial success, they were driven back. This proved the close of active operations for the year, as nothing further of importance took place in this department. Our army was rapidly filling up from the recent conscription, while the South had already reached its last ditch. It had no reserve force to call upon, its resources were becoming exhausted, and its army reduced to extremities.

About this time our regiment received some forty or more recruits, and for the week that followed, until December 7, it remained in the vicinity of Deep Bottom. Its routine of duties is indicated by a single day's record, taken from the journal of Townsend — date, November 8. "In the morning, at four o'clock, we were turned out, and went inside the fort, and remained until seven o'clock, and were then dismissed. The weather being clear, after breakfast we were all ordered on fatigue; some building log huts, and the rest in the woods carrying logs. We worked all day, and at six o'clock in the afternoon were dismissed." On

OFFICERS' QUARTERS, CHAPIN'S FARM.

the 15th, the huts were completed, tents were taken down, and the regiment went into winter-quarters.

The 24th was Thanksgiving Day, to be specially remembered by every soldier on account of the abundant supply of turkeys, apples, and other good things, furnished them by the people of the North, and distributed through the agency of the two societies previously referred to. Through this period, squad, company, and battalion drills were kept up with as much regularity as relief from other duties permitted. The size of the regiment may be inferred from the fact that five companies were usually united for a company drill.

December 3, Colonel Barton, having reached the limit of his term of service, was mustered out at his own request. The inconvenience resulting from the wounds received at Fort Wagner and Cold Harbor, and his general condition of physical prostration, demanded a rest. He had proved an earnest, faithful, efficient, and intelligent officer, and the regiment, under his command, attained a proficiency in drill and a condition of general excellence that easily placed it at the head of the troops with which it was associated. Often detached on special important service, he filled every position with credit to himself and satisfaction to his superior officers. His relations with the commanding officers under whom we served in the several departments were

PONTOON BRIDGE AT JONES' LANDING, NEAR DEEP BOTTOM.

uniformly of an agreeable character, a circumstance from which the regiment profited to no inconsiderable extent. His brevet of brigadier-general was well earned, and he may well regard the years of service which he gave to his country as entitling him to general respect and esteem. On the 5th of December, all the white troops of the 10th and 18th corps were consolidated and formed the 24th, and the colored troops from the same formed the 25th corps.

On the evening of the 6th, orders were received to pack up and be ready for a march, but the movement did not take place until the afternoon of the 7th, when the 2d division, to which our regiment was assigned, formed in line and started for Jones' Landing, near City Point, where they arrived on the morning of the 8th. Here they embarked on the steamer Perritt, and proceeded to Fortress Monroe, the point of rendezvous of the expedition. On the 13th they left Fortress Monroe, and for much of the time until the 30th were steaming up and down the coast. For several days they were at Beaufort. N. C., taking in supplies of coal and water, and from there proceeded to Cape Fear River, and landed near Fort Fisher, intending to make an assault; but General Weitzel, who had immediate command of the troops, declared it would be suicidal to make the attempt, and the men re-embarked, and the transports returned directly to City Point.

General Butler, who had charge of the land forces, conceived the idea of sending in near to Fort Fisher a vessel loaded with powder, expecting that by its explosion the fort would be materially damaged. The plan was carried out, but no visible effect followed the explosion, and the expedition, which was based upon the success of the plan, proved a failure. From City Point the regiment returned to its old position at Chapin's Farm. The men had suffered from their long confinement on the dirty steamer. The food was insufficient and the vermin intolerable, and it was a blessed relief to get back where they could cleanse and purify themselves and clothing.

From December 30 to January 3 they were allowed to remain in camp, enjoying quiet and rest. On that day everything was packed and made ready for a change, in obedience to orders, and on the evening of the 3d they started for Bermuda Hundred. On the 4th, they embarked on the steamer Tonawanda, and the next day were at Fortress Monroe. On the 8th they were in Hatteras Inlet. On the 9th, they joined the fleet off Beaufort, N. C. On the 12th, they were in Cape Fear River, and on the 13th moved farther in, and nearer Fort Fisher.

A change had been made. General Butler had been relieved on his return from the former expedition, and General A. H. Terry was now in command of the troops, while Admiral Porter commanded the naval forces, as before. At ten o'clock on the morning of the 13th, a landing was effected in small boats, and the troops formed on the beach and stacked arms, and proceeded to throw up intrenchments from Cape Fear River to the beach. During the 13th and 14th, a heavy bombardment was kept up on Fort Fisher by the navy, and on the 15th our division, which had been working round to the rear of the fort, prepared for an assault.

Having left behind knapsacks and all other encumbrances, about two o'clock in the afternoon the first charge was made, which resulted in securing the outer section of the fort. At the same time, the naval brigade charged in front. Charge succeeded charge, until ten o'clock in the evening, when the garrison, having been driven into our bastion, surrendered. The fighting on both sides was very stubborn. From the description of the fort, which I gather from those present at the assault, it was composed of detached mounds. When one was taken, our men gathered behind it for a short halt and rest. And then, with a sudden rush and bound over and around this mound, another was taken, until at last the whole was captured, with twenty-five hundred prisoners and sixty guns. Our losses were quite severe. Captain Dunn, my old orderly sergeant, who behaved so well at Chester Heights, was killed; and many names in our regiment, as well as in the others engaged, were added to the long list of martyrs. Everything had been arranged to blow up the fort, rather than surrender it; but the wires connecting the batteries which were arranged to effect the explosion were cut off from their connections with the magazines by the shot and shell from the navy. A slight explosion did take place, late at night, after our regiment had been withdrawn. Several other small forts in the vicinity were blown up by the Confederates, but the garrison of Fort Anderson, some little distance up the river, remained in possession until February 19, when the disposition of our troops was such that there could no longer be any hope of being able to hold it, and it was evacuated.

INTERIOR OF FORT FISHER.

During the interval, our forces had been strengthened, by the arrival of the 23d army corps, under General Schofield, and many new recruits had arrived from the North, our regiment receiving on the 7th of February two hundred and ten.

The capture of Fort Fisher was an important event. By it one of the worst points on the southern coast was shut up, for, in spite of the utmost vigilance on the part of our navy, immense quantities of supplies had been brought in, through the several entrances of Cape Fear River, by blockade-runners. But a much more important service was rendered to our cause by its capture than in cutting off supplies. For at this time General Sherman, having completed the wonderful march from Atlanta to the sea-coast at Savannah, had now turned northward, and was on his way to co-operate with the Army of Virginia, in that final struggle which ended the rebellion; and the capture of Fort Fisher, and the other defences on Cape Fear River gave a new basis of supplies and military operations, which materially aided Sherman.

General Terry, having succeeded in capturing these forts, disposed his forces, which consisted of about eight thousand men, in such a manner

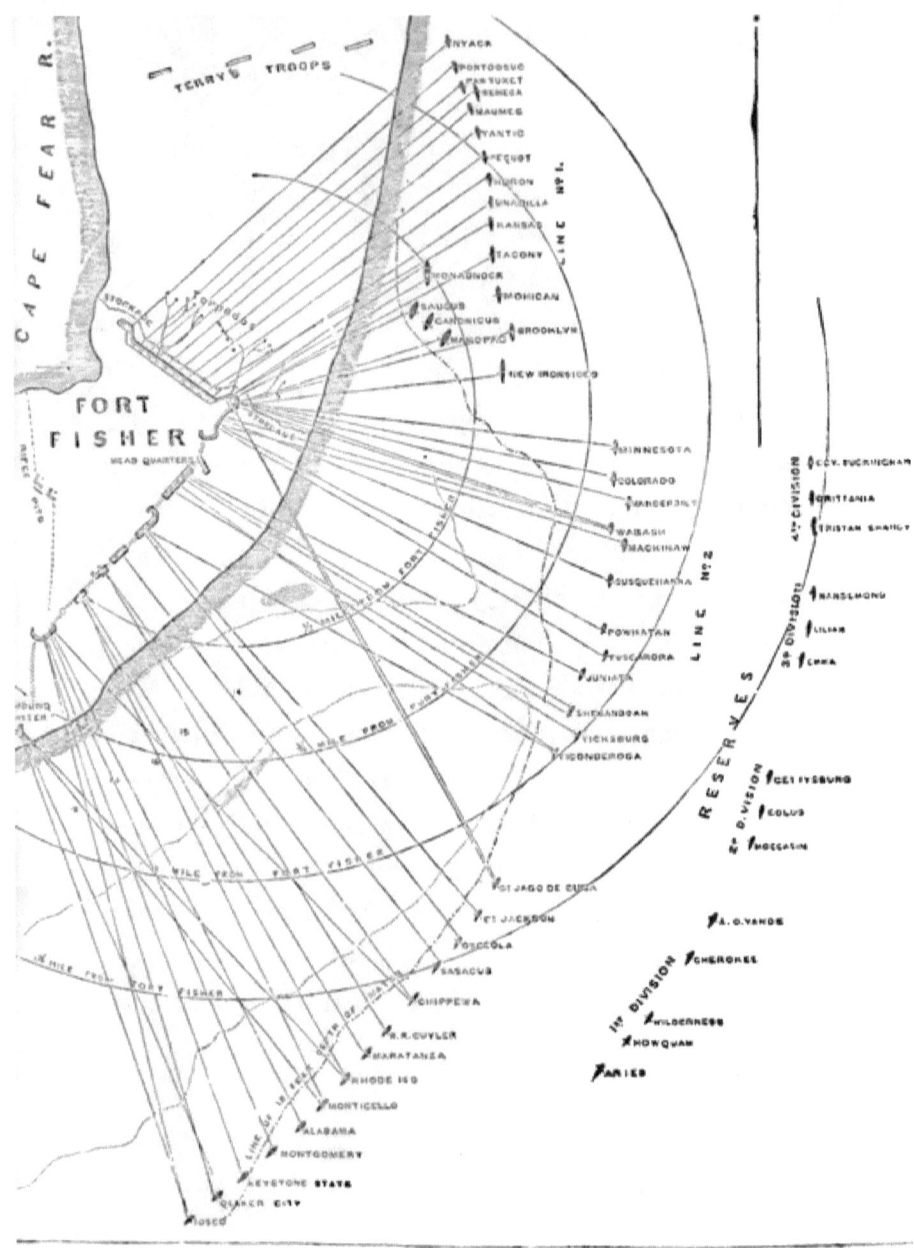

PLAN OF LAND AND NAVAL OPERATIONS AT FORT FISHER.

as to be secure from attacks, and awaited the action of General Schofield, who had been assigned the command of the new department of North Carolina. No time was wasted. New and more favorable positions were taken from time to time, and on the 20th a general movement was made towards Wilmington.

On the 21st, our regiment, which, with the other troops under General Terry, was advancing towards this city on the east side of the river, suddenly came upon a strong force of the Confederates, who opened a heavy fire, by which two men were killed, and Major Elfwing and seventeen others wounded. The enemy were driven within their works and held there, until a division under General Cox, by threatening to cross the river above the city, compelled a general retreat, which was effected after the burning of the steamers at the wharves, and the destruction of the military stores and cotton in and near the city.

On the 22d, Washington's birthday, Wilmington was occupied by our troops, and perhaps no result of this occupation was of as much interest to the soldiers as the fact that by it they secured a supply of tobacco, of which they had been deprived for several weeks. In the recent operations, the loss to the Federal side was about two hundred in killed, wounded, and missing; and the Confederate loss, about a thousand, in killed and wounded, while a large number of prisoners, with thirty pieces of cannon, and an immense quantity of ammunition, had fallen into our hands.

General Schofield's next movement was against Goldsboro, to open a communication with General Sherman; and a large force was sent to Kingston, to secure and repair the railroad. These troops advanced by way of Newbern. Our division was allowed no rest, but on the afternoon of the 22d started in pursuit of the retreating enemy. So sharply was this kept up that on the 27th a flag of truce was proposed by the Confederate commander, for the purpose of transferring the Union prisoners, so much did they encumber his movements. Accordingly, we received into our lines nearly ten thousand, officers and privates, some of whom had been captured from our regiment at

MOUND BATTERY, NEAR FORT FISHER.

Olustee and Cold Harbor. All were in the most deplorable condition, half clothed and almost wholly starved. These were conveyed to Wilmington, to which city our regiment returned March 2.

New recruits arrived from time to time, and were instructed in their duties, and, with the exception of one short expedition to guard wagon-trains, the regiment remained near Wilmington until the 15th.

March 12, General Sherman, who had arrived at Fayetteville, sent despatches to General Schofield, directing him to march at once to Goldsboro, and to order General Terry to do the same. Accordingly, on the 15th they broke camp, and started to join Sherman. That night, before they lay down, they had marched twenty-five miles. The following day the march was resumed, and, although the roads were very heavy, they moved rapidly, and day after day continued on, with no special accident, or incident, until the 21st, when signs of Sherman's bummers began to appear, and in the afternoon there was heavy cannonading on our left.

At this time, and for some time previous, our troops had subsisted largely by foraging. Sugar and coffee were almost forgotten luxuries.

On the the 23d, the 17th corps of Sherman's army passed near our troops, and the motley procession which accompanied them showed how successful they had become as foragers. Goldsboro had been taken by General Schofield's troops on the 21st, and Johnston had massed his army at Smithfield. General Sherman had now a large force under his command, and, with several good safe bases of supplies, and uninterrupted communication with the coast, was prepared to perform his part in these final struggles of the rebellion. His march from Savannah had resulted in the loss to the Confederates of all the fortified points along the coast, with the immense quantities of supplies and materials of war which they contained. A tract of fifty miles in width, along his whole route, had been stripped of all kinds of provisions, and the richest portion of the South had been devastated. The great system of internal communication and supply, which had afforded them such great advantages in the movements of their armies, was either destroyed or fatally disarranged.

By this time General Grant was ready for that final movement against Lee which resulted in the surrender of his army. This movement commenced on the 29th, and, after repeated attempts upon the enemy's right, a general assault, along the whole line, on April 2, resulted in complete success, and on the morning of the 3d it was discovered that Lee's army had fled, and on that day our troops, under General Weitzel, occupied Richmond. The principal part of Grant's army passed on after Lee. Sheridan, with his whole force of cavalry, by rapid marches, finally succeeded, on the 9th, in intercepting Lee's retreat, and, by a vigorous attack, held him in check until the arrival of several corps of infantry made escape impossible; and on that day Lee. and what remained of his army, fell into our hands. The principal army now remaining to the Confederates was that commanded by Johnston.

General Sherman, while these operations were going on, was resting at Goldsboro; but on the 11th orders came from General Grant to move against Johnston. As late as March 28, new recruits were received from the North, nearly a hundred and fifty being assigned to our regiment; and when, on the 11th, General Sherman broke camp and started for Johnston, it was with an army invigorated, strengthened, and refreshed, and stimulated to unbounded enthusiasm by the success of the Army of Virginia. April 6, general orders had been promulgated to all the troops at their evening parades, stating that Petersburg and Richmond had been taken, and that Lee was retreating.

April 7, another despatch was read, announcing that General Sheridan had captured twelve thousand prisoners and fifty pieces of artillery. On the 10th, two divisions of the 10th corps, which had again been reunited under General Terry, started on the march towards Raleigh. On the 11th, the march was continued rapidly, our brigade being in the advance. Frequent halts were necessary, on account of the destruction of the bridges by Johnston's army. On the 12th, while resting and waiting for a wagon-train, for which they were to be escort, a despatch was read from General Schofield announcing the surrender of General Lee. This had been known by other portions of the army, which had passed

M'LEAN'S HOUSE, THE PLACE OF LEE'S SURRENDER.

on from other points, and had already driven Johnston's army out of Smithfield.

The forward movement was resumed by our brigade on the afternoon of the 12th, but the roads continued very heavy, and the men were often compelled to wade through swamps, and at night slept on the ground with scarcely more than the sky for a covering. On the evening of the 14th, they arrived in the vicinity of Raleigh, and established camp a short distance outside the city. The Confederate army had made no stop here, and General Sherman continued the pursuit some twenty or twenty-five miles, to a point called Durham Station, when, the hopelessness of further resistance being apparent, a request was sent to General Sherman by Johnston, asking for a truce, with a view to arranging the terms of surrender of his army. This occurred on the 15th, and as the fact became generally known on the 16th, that night was given up to rejoicing, for it was felt that the war was now over. This, however, proved premature, for the terms proposed, and which were evidently dictated by Davis and other leaders of the rebellion, who were known to be in the vicinity, although accepted by General Sherman, when submitted to the authorities at Washington, were unhesitatingly repudiated as dealing with questions which were beyond the province of military commanders; and orders were issued to resume operations at once. General Grant was despatched to Raleigh, where he arrived on the 24th, and notice was sent to Johnston demanding an immediate surrender, on the same terms given to General Lee. The troops were

PLACE OF JOHNSTON'S SURRENDER TO SHERMAN.

put in motion, and preparations were made to reopen the campaign; and it is safe to say that no order was ever issued to our troops which was received with such universal satisfaction as that to prepare to march against Johnston. News had been received of the assassination of President Lincoln, and, had our troops encountered Johnston's army, no quarter would have been given, so terribly were they exasperated. But, fortunately for Johnston and those under him, wise counsels prevailed in his camp, and on the 26th his whole army was surrendered, and the war was virtually over.

CHAPTER XIX.

A general review. Change in condition of the regiment. Barrett as provost-marshal. Delicate question. Colonel Coan. Gradual disbandment of the army. Discharge of the 48th. Some personal explanations.

LITTLE remains to chronicle in the history of the 48th. On the 20th of April, during the truce between the two armies, a general review was held in Raleigh by General Sherman. The 10th corps presented no such appearance as when it marched in review at Hilton Head. Few of the old officers and soldiers were left, and the experiences of the past year had been such as to preclude the possibility of keeping up that almost perfect condition and discipline for which we were so long noted. Our regiment had changed so much that it bore its share of the censure contained in general orders issued a few nights after the review. But sufficient allowance was not made for the peculiar hardships and exposures of the recent campaign, nor for the addition of so many new recruits, at a time when no opportunity was afforded for their proper training and drill. The work of all the troops was done and well done, and no censure should have mingled with the approval they so richly deserved.

After the surrender of Johnston, our brigade, commanded by Colonel Coan, remained in Raleigh, until sent home to be discharged from the service. Captain Barrett, now commissioned major, but unable to be mustered in, on account of the wound of Major Elfwing, which prevented his advancement, was made provost-marshal. The duties of the position were varied and peculiar, but, exercising that excellent good sense and kindly disposition which always characterized him, he gave general satisfaction. It must have been a little embarrassing when he was called upon to settle the question between the negro and his two wives. Having been separated from the object of his early affections, by change of ownership, the negro had found another to solace and comfort him, with whom he had been living some twenty years, and the sudden appearance of wife number one with a request that he should resume his former relations involved questions too deep for his understanding. The decision of the provost-marshal, that possession for so long a time established the right to hold, and that number one must continue to regard the separation as final, as she had done for so long a period of years, was satisfactory, at least to the negro and wife number two.

The order announcing that Johnston had surrendered, and that the troops would soon be marching homewards, was published April 27; but it was found no simple matter to disband so large an army, and, while no further hostilities were feared, there were many questions to be decided, arising out of the war, which required the presence of troops in the South.

The weeks and months which followed brought to the regiment little change from the regular round of guard and fatigue duty, inspections and parades. Coan, who was a captain of the regiment at its organization in 1861, was now its colonel. Almost the only one of the original officers who remained with the regiment, he had served constantly and faithfully through the intervening years, and was finally mustered out with it. In every position which he occupied, whether commanding a company, the regiment, or a brigade, he always did his part well, and enjoyed the confidence and respect of every one. He had no enemies, because he always exercised the authority entrusted to him with good judgment and a due consideration for others. Sharing hardships and dangers equally with others, he was wonderfully spared, having never suffered seriously from sickness or wounds. His services on earth are now ended, but his memory is fondly cherished by all who knew him.

June 10, the remnant of the 117th New York State Volunteers was consolidated with our regiment, which became nearly complete in numbers, both of officers and privates. June 19, the 48th escorted the 115th New York to the depot, on their way home to become citizens again, and on the 23d, performed a similar duty for the 203d Pennsylvania Volunteers, which had been brigaded with it for many months.

On the 26th, the regiment was considerably reduced, by the mustering-out of all those whose term of service would expire before

September. From this time onwards the story of the journals before us is a dull and unvaried account of simple and uninteresting details, which continues until August 31, when the regiment was mustered out of the service of the United States. On Sunday, September 3, it started in the cars for City Point, where it took steamer for Baltimore. September 5, it arrived in New York city, and on the following day was conveyed to Hart's Island, where it remained encamped until the 12th. On that day, the pay roll was signed for the last time, the regiment was discharged, and the men were transported to New York city, free and independent citizens once more.

This completes the history of the struggles and triumphs of "the Saints," so far as it could be gleaned from the materials at hand. The assistance received from the several journals sent me I have already acknowledged, but while drawing as largely as possible from these, I have been compelled to rely to a great extent upon my own. This was kept with constancy and regularity from day to day, during my whole term of service, and has been useful not only in furnishing such facts of our daily experience as it contained, but also in recalling by its perusal much that was unrecorded which has come back to me from the sleeping recesses of memory. If out of this great dependence upon a personal narrative there appears more of the individual than is seemly and proper, I beg, especially from those who participated in the scenes depicted, a charitable construction of this natural if not necessary tendency, and that I be absolved from any intention to give to my own special services undue prominence.

CHAPTER XX.

Special references to some of the officers of the regiment. Remarks upon prominent questions before the country. Finis.

OF some of those who were my companions during the progress of the war I have made mention, but in the final review of narrative I am reminded of many others whom I have omitted, to whose worth I could testify with earnestness and feeling. I am conscious, also, of not having given sufficient prominence to the social life in the army. Our duties were oftentimes severe, trying, and perilous; but it was not all duty, and my intercourse with many if not most of the officers whom I met was both elevating and stimulating, especially within our own regiment. I remember well my first introduction to Captain (afterwards Lieutenant-Colonel) Strickland. He was officer of the day when I made my first application to be admitted to the camp at Fort Hamilton. "What are you here for?" he asked, to which I replied that I hoped to become an officer of the regiment. "Impossible!" said he, "and I advise you to take yourself off as quickly as possible, as every officer has been selected, and there isn't a ghost of a chance for you." Further explanation, however, effected an entrance to the camp; and before the guard was relieved I had been regularly mustered into the service, as second lieutenant of Company G. Notwithstanding the brusqueness of his first salutation, I found him to be an educated gentleman, and my relations with him while he remained in the service were intimate and most agreeable. Of Lockwood I have already written, but have only faintly expressed the constant pleasure which I enjoyed in his companionship. Hurst and Edwards, both sacrificed at Wagner, although of diverse habits and tastes, contributed their full share to the social life of the regiment, while Carleton, Miller and Bodine are all living to enjoy the memory of their faithful service in camp and field. Among the younger officers was Dr. J. Mott Throop, assistant surgeon. I could not forget him; for, while lying in the hospital, stricken down with fever, he brought me the welcome papers which made me free again. Better than medicine had been his friendly offices; but better than all else combined was the release from army life when there could be no hope of restoration to health, and consequently no further efficient service. In all the world he could find no lovelier scenes than now surround him in his home among the Berkshire Hills. As he goes his daily round of ministration to the sick and suffering, may the beauty which appeals to him from hill and mountain side and peaceful valley minister to his soul continual comfort and joy, is the sincere wish of his friend and former comrade. Now, having told my story and rendered these forgotten tributes, I seem to hear the patient reader who has followed me to this point say: Why don't he add the finis and have done. So perhaps I should. But may I not be indulged in a few reflections which seem to claim a relationship with the events herein narrated? Since the surrender at Appomattox, another generation has arisen, and many of those who were too young to participate in, or even understand, the questions involved in the war have grown to manhood and are occupying places in the State and National councils. The war is indeed over, but to these, and to all others who aspire to official positions, — yes, and equally to the people at large, — there remain duties to perform, difficulties and perils to encounter. Not so great, it may be, as those here narrated, but such as shall test the loyalty and patriotism as surely if not so severely as in the scenes herein depicted. The colored people of the South have been endowed with the full rights of citizenship under the law; but the task remains of fitting them for the exercise of this great privilege, and protecting them against injustice and wrong. Under the influence of a discontented and vicious class of emigrants from the old world who have brought from its oppressions and want a spirit of rebellion against even the most necessary restraints of society, serious divisions have been created. The poorer and those who call themselves the laboring class have arrayed themselves in organized antagonism against those more sagacious and more successful than themselves. The cry of the communist of Paris is being repeated here and must be heeded, or the most unhappy results may follow. May we rest, then, in blind security, or shall the men of this and coming generations rather emulate the spirit of their fathers who, with true devotion to principle and duty, freely offered all, even life itself, on the altar of their country? Let the questions which now occupy the minds of the people be settled on the broadest principles of justice. Let every wrong that now disturbs the peace and well-being of society be met and adjusted, with the fullest regard for the welfare of the humblest and most dependent, and may the spirit which animated the "Saints" be the promise and fulfilment of the hopes and prayers of those who sought these shores whereon to found a government which should guarantee to all men freedom, justice, and equality.

www.ingramcontent.com/pod-product-compliance
Lightning Source LLC
Chambersburg PA
CBHW030815230426
43667CB00008B/1226